실전 해외관광과 영어실력 향상을 동시에

TOURISM ENGLISH A to Z

신동선·박상현 공저

 백산출판사

Preface

영어는 만국공통어(lingua franca)가 되고 있으며 특히 해외 관광을 할 때 필수 요소가 되고 있다. 이에 따라 관광 관련 학과에서는 관광영어 과목을 개설하여 학생들이 관광 종사원으로서 그리고 해외 관광자로서 원활한 의사소통을 하도록 훈련하고 있다.

어떤 교재를 선택하느냐에 따라 수업의 내용이 달라질 수 있는데 국내에 출판된 대부분의 교재는 관광에서 일어날 수 있는 상황별로 대화를 반복 연습(drilling)하는 형태로 되어 있다. 그러나 학생들의 욕구를 조사해 본 결과 단순히 몇 개의 문장을 암기하는 것에서 벗어나 영어 능력 자체를 향상시키고 싶어 한다는 것을 알 수 있었다. 수업 방식도 말하기(speaking)에 초점을 둔 의사소통중심교수법(communicative language teaching)을 선호하고 있었다.

따라서 본 교재는 이러한 연구결과와 저자들의 다년간의 교육 경험을 바탕으로 우리나라 관광 관련 학과 학생들에게 적합하도록 설계되었으며 다음과 같은 특징을 갖는다.

* 매 장마다 영어의 4대 기술(skill)인 말하기(speaking), 듣기(listening), 읽기(reading), 쓰기(writing) 능력을 향상할 수 있도록 하였다.
* 각 장은 처음 여행을 시작하면서부터 여행사, 공항, 호텔, 식당, 관광지 등 해외 관광에서 일어날 수 있는 상황을 순서대로 연습할 수 있도록 하였다.
* 각 장의 기술(skill)별 본문 내용은 서로 밀접한 연관을 갖고 있기 때문에 4대 기술을 연습하는 과정에서 상황에 필요한 영어를 자연스럽게 연습하도록 하였다.
* 단어에 있어서도 단순히 암기하는 것이 아니라 단어 맞추기 퀴즈를 통해 재미있게 단어를 추측(guess)하는 능력을 향상할 수 있고, 본문에 대한 기대감을 갖게 되고, 본문을 통해 그 단어를 사용하면서 실제 문장 중에서 어떻게 사용되는지 습득하도록 하였다.
* 교재의 모든 문장을 영어로 작성하여 학생들이 수업 중에 온전히 영어에만 노출

되도록 하였다. 같은 패턴이 반복되므로 처음에 익숙하지 않았던 학생도 금방 적응할 수 있으며 갈수록 영어 능력이 향상되는 것을 느낄 수 있다.

＊우리나라 학생들의 영어 능력을 고려하여 교재의 수준을 upper beginner에서 intermediate로 정하였다.

＊교수자의 입장에서도 각 장마다 다양한 activity가 포함되어 있으므로 active한 수업을 진행할 수 있다.

본 교재를 통해서 우리나라 학생들의 관광영어 능력과 영어 능력이 동시에 향상되기를 희망하며 앞으로 관광 종사원으로서 외국 관광객에게 원활한 서비스를 제공하고 본인의 해외 관광 시에도 언어의 문제없이 즐겁게 여행하면서 많은 친구를 사귀고 견문을 넓힐 수 있길 기원한다.

저자 신동선·박상현

Contents

Unit

1

At travel agency:

Counselling on Itineraries

Building Vocabulary

Match the words with the same meaning.

1. consultant •

• ⓐ from or in another country, especially a tropical one; seeming exciting and unusual because it is connected with foreign countries

2. ad •

• ⓑ if something costs a particular amount of money, you need to pay that amount in order to buy, make or do it

3. on the Internet •

• ⓒ a small magazine or book containing pictures and information about something or advertising something

4. get married •

• ⓓ through the Internet

5. exotic •

• ⓔ as good as or better than others

6. highly •

• ⓕ advertisement

7. recommend •

• ⓖ to tell somebody that something is good or useful, or that somebody would be suitable for a particular job, etc.

8. cost •

• ⓗ to have a husband or wife

9. competitive •

• ⓘ a person who knows a lot about a particular subject and is employed to give advice about it to other people

10. brochure •

• ⓙ very

Reading an Article

Read the itinerary and answer the following questions.

NORTHERN ODYSSEY TOUR DEPARTING SEPT.9

For your convenience, we recommend that you check your luggage through to Helsinki, Finland. Please wear your NORTHERN ODYSSEY TOUR badge during transfers to facilitate identification by our representatives.

(SAT. SEPT.9)   **DEPART USA** via air

(Please refer to your personal air itineraries for departure / arrival times.)

(SUN. SEPT.10)   **ARRIVE HELSINKI, FINLAND**

Accommodations : Presidenti Hotel

(TUE. SEPT.12)   **DEPART HELSINKI** motorcoach to dock

Accommodations : SS Northern Lights

(FRI. SEPT.15)   **ARRIVE STOCKHOLM, SWEDEN** via ship

Accommodations : Royal Viking Hotel

(MON. SEPT.18)   **DEPART STOCKHOLM** via Air Scandinavia

ARRIVE COPENHAGEN, DENMARK

Accommodations : Air Scandinavia Hotel

(SAT. SEPT.23)   **DEPART COPENHAGEN** via Air Scandinavia

ARRIVE OSLO, NORWAY

Accommodations : Princess Christiana Hotel

(WED. SEPT.27)   **DEPART OSLO** via railroad

ARRIVE BERGEN, NORWAY

Accommodations : Hotel Bryggen

DEPART BERGEN by air

ARRIVE USA

(Please refer to your personal air itineraries. All passengers are required to clear U.S. Customs.)

1 Why are the members of the tour asked to wear badges?

(a) To get seats on the plane

(b) To be recognized by tour representatives

(c) To get through customs quickly

(d) to recognize each other easily

2 How will members of the tour go form Helsinki to Stockholm?

(a) By motorcoach   (b) By air

(c) By train   (d) By ship

3 In which of these cities will members of the tour spend the most time?

(a) Copenhagen   (b) Stockholm

(c) Bergen   (d) Helsinki

4 How long will the entire tour take?

(a) 1week   (b) 2weeks

(c) 3weeks   (d) 4weeks

Grammar Tips

like + -ing

like + to + the base form of Verb

would like to + the base form of Verb

After verb "like" you can use ⟨to + the base form of Verb⟩ or ⟨-ing⟩.

(1) We normally use ⟨-ing⟩ for a situation that already exists or existed.

ex. Ryan teaches biology. He likes it. He <u>likes teaching</u> biology.

(2) In other situations, you can use ⟨to + the base form of Verb⟩ or ⟨-ing⟩.
But ⟨to + the base form of Verb⟩ is more usual.

ex. I don't <u>like to write</u> letters. I can never think what to write. (O)

I don't <u>like writing</u> letters. I can never think what to write. (O)

(3) We can use more "would like to" than "like" in particular situation.

ex. I <u>would like to</u> play tennis today. (= I want to play today)

I <u>like playing</u> tennis. OR I <u>like to play</u> tennis. (= I enjoy it in general)

Write an appropriate verb in the correct form, ⟨-ing⟩ or ⟨to + the base form of Verb⟩. Sometimes either form is possible.

1 I would love _____ to your wedding, but I'm afraid I can't.

2 Caroline never wears a hat. She doesn't like _____ hats.

3 "Would you like _____ down?" "No, thanks. I'll stand."

4 I don't like _____ in this part of town. I want to live somewhere else.

5 Do you have a minute? I'd like _____ to you about something.

Listening Spot
Listen to a Conversation

Try to complete the conversation with expressions from the chart below. Then listen and check your answers.

Travel Consultant : Hello, can I help you?

Rita : I saw your ads on the Internet and **1**_____

Travel Consultant : **2**_____

Rita : I'm getting married and **3**_____

Travel Consultant : In that case, I highly recommend Bali for you. When do you plan to go?

Rita	: 4_____
Travel Consultant	: How long do you want to stay?
Rita	: About a week. How much does it cost?
Travel Consultant	: Well, it's very competitive. 5_____
Rita	: Yes, please. Thank you.

I'd like to be there next month.

I'd like to get some information.

I'd like to go somewhere exotic.

Where would you like to go?

Would you like a brochure?

Listening Tips

Contraction is a short form of a word. The examples are as follow:

I'm = I am / He's = He is / She's = She is / They're = They are

What's = What is / Where's = Where is

I'd like = I would like / I'd like to = I would like to

He's been = He has been / won't = will not

Listen and put a check(✓) next to the sentence you hear.

1 □ They're from Brazil.

  □ There's from Brazil.

2 □ He's a teacher in Italy.

  □ His teacher in Italy.

3 □ I like to play the piano.

  □ I'd like to play the piano.

4 □ He is been in Australia for three years.

  □ He's been in Australia for three years.

5 ☐ It won't be held in Paris.

☐ It will be held in Paris.

Further
Listening

Listen the following each conversation and choose the answer.

1 How will the woman travel?

(a) By bus
(b) By boat

(c) By plane
(d) By train

2 How does the man feel?

(a) Excited
(b) Calm

(c) Unhappy
(d) Nervous

3 Where does the woman feel closed in?

(a) In elevators
(b) In dark theaters

(c) In phone booths
(d) In airplanes

4−5 Where is the caller calling from?

(a) From Paris

(b) From outside Paris

(c) It is not clear from the message.

(d) From a country other than France

What is the caller advised to do?

(a) Press a number

(b) Hang up and call again

(c) Telephone for information

(d) Wait for an operator to answer

Role-play

When do you plan to go?	**Next month.**
How long do you want to stay?	**About a week.**
How much does it cost?	**It's very competitive.**

○————

When do you plan to go?	I plan to go next Friday.
When are you planning to go?	I am planning to go tomorrow.
When do you want to go?	I want to go next year.
When would you like to go?	I would like to go someday.

○————

How long do you want to stay?	I want to stay for three weeks.
How long would you like to stay?	I would like to stay for a month.
How long are you going to stay?	I am going to stay for five days.
How long do you plan to stay?	I plan to stay for half a year.

○————

How much does it cost?	It depends.
How much is it?	It's very resonable.
	It's very affordable.

Conversation Tips

"Well" is often used by English speaker to begin responses.

A : How much does it cost?

B : <u>Well</u>, it's very competitive.

ex. A : What do you think?

　　B : <u>Well</u>, maybe the reason is. . .

ex. A : How did you like the movie?

B : <u>Well</u>, I thought it was disappointing.

Writing Tips

Would like / would love / would hate / would prefer are usually followed by ⟨**to + the base form of the Verb**⟩.

ex. I <u>would like to be</u> rich.

<u>Would</u> you <u>like to come</u> to dinner on Friday?

I'<u>d love to be</u> able to travel around the world.

<u>Would</u> you <u>prefer to have</u> dinner now or later?

Do It Yourself

Complete the sentences using the following words.

1 buy / one-way

I would like _____ .

2 stay / three days

I would like _____ .

3 travel / with sister

I would like _____ .

4 go / London

I would like _____ .

5 make / a few stops

I would like_____.

6 get / information

I would like_____.

7 leave / next Friday

I would like_____.

Unit

2

At travel agency:

Making a Flight Reservation

Building Vocabulary

Match the words with the same meaning.

1. return •
    • ⓐ to find out if something is correct or true or if something is how you think it is

2. flight •
    • ⓑ a journey to a place and back again

3. check •
    • ⓒ the part of a plane where passengers have a high level of comfort and service, designed for people travelling on business, and less expensive than first class

4. available •
    • ⓓ that you can get, buy or find

5. one-way •
    • ⓔ a place where you pay to sit in a plane, train, theatre, ect.

6. round trip •
    • ⓕ the best and most expensive seats or accommodation on a train, plane or ship

7. seat •
    • ⓖ to come or go back from one place to another

8. economy class •
    • ⓗ a plane making a particular journey

9. business class •
    • ⓘ tourist class

10. first class •
    • ⓙ moving or allowing movement in only one direction

Reading an Article

Read the letter and answer the following questions.

Dear Bob,

I am flying back to Vancouver from Seoul the day after tomorrow, with two potential clients. They represent a Korean firm new to the Canadian market and Canadian law and are interested in using our services to assist them with their planned investments in British Columbia.

Please have Sally make reservations at the Vancouver Royalto, three singles / seven days, as well as reservations at the Lido for dinner on the 16th.

I probably will not be in touch again, unless the situation changes. Many thanks.

Yours,

Ellen

1 Where is the woman flying to?

    (a) Lido   (b) Seoul

    (c) Vancouver   (d) Great Britain

2 What does the woman want done?

    (a) She wants reservations made.

    (b) She want to retain a lawyer.

    (c) She wants a meeting room set up.

    (d) She wants her guests to meet Sally.

3 When will the writer be returning?

    (a) Within two days   (b) On the 16th

    (c) After meeting two more clients   (d) She does not say.

here be + Subject

There is a telephone.

There are three plants.

(1) Affirmative

  ex. There <u>is</u> a television.

    There <u>are</u> some books.

(2) Negative

  ex. There <u>isn't</u> a radio.

    There <u>aren't</u> any photographs.

(3) Question

  ex. <u>Is</u> there a radio?

    <u>Are</u> there any books?

Read and complete the answers.

1 Is there a television? Yes, there _____.

2 Is there a radio? No, there _____.

3 Are there any books? Yes, there _____.

4 How many books are there? There _____ a lot.

5 Are there any photographs? No, there _____.

Listen to a Conversation

Try to complete the conversation with expressions from the chart below. Then listen and check your answers.

Travel Consultant : Good afternoon, how can I help you?

Emma : I'd like to fly to Bali with my husband on October 14th and return on October 20th.

Travel Consultant : What time do you want to leave?

Emma : 1_____

Travel Consultant : OK, I'll check if the flight is available.

2_____

Emma : Round trip, please.

Travel Consultant : (Pause) Thank you for waiting, ma'am.

3_____ Economy class or first class, ma'am?

Emma : Economy class, please.

Travel Consultant : 4_____

Emma : Emma Nelson, 010-3212-2588.

Travel Consultant : All right. 5_____

Emma : Yes, thank you.

Do you want to pay for it now?

Is there a flight around 7:00 o'clock in the evening?

May I have your name and phone number, please?

There are some seats available at that time.

Will you be flying one-way or round trip?

Listening Tips

Look at the words. What are a, e, i, o, and u?

Why do you pronounce the differently depending on the situations?

the[ðə]	the[ði]
the bag	the apple
the ticket	the orange
the letter	the English book
in the morning	in the evening
the one	the hour
	the honor
	the umbrella

Listen and put a check(✓) next to the sentence you hear.

1 □ Look at this house over there!

   □ Look at the house over there!

2 □ Henry, this is my mother. Mom, this is Henry.

   □ Henry, there is my mother. Mom, there is Henry.

3 □ This is very useful equipment.

   □ This is very used equipment.

4 □ Did you see Jane last week?

   □ You see Jane last week?

5 □ Did you get the job?

   □ Did you got the job?

Listen the following each conversation and choose the answer.

1 Why will the man be charged extra?

(a) He wants room service.

(b) He wants the penthouse.

(c) He wants a room with a view.

(d) He wants flowers and fruit in his room.

2 What did the man want to do?

(a) Change his seat

(b) Take an earlier flight

(c) Exchange his airplane ticket

(d) Smoke on board the airplane

3–5 Why would you press 1?

(a) If you have a rotary phone

(b) To show down the recording

(c) To speed up your call

(d) If you want to check airfares

Which number do you select to hear arrival and departure information?

(a) 1   (b) 2

(c) 4   (d) 5

What special service does Ansett Airlines offer?

(a) Repeated telephone menus

(b) Flights to Canada and the Caribbean

(c) Flyaway Vacations

(d) Ticket delivery

Role-play

Is there a coffee mug?	Yes, there is a black one on the table.
Is there a telephone?	No, there isn't.

Are there any cushions?	Yes, there are two next to the sofa.
	No, there aren't.

Ask and answer questions about these things.

a cat	pictures
a piano	plants
a balcony	clocks
a rug	newspapers
a mirror	flowers
a computer	bookshelves
a lamp	photos
a coffee table	magazines
an armchair	cushions
a sofa	dogs

Conversation Tip

"Please" is often used by English speaker to ask for politely.

A : Will you be flying one-way or round trip?

B : Round trip, <u>please</u>.

A : Economy class or first class, ma'am?

B : Economy class, <u>please</u>.

ex. A : Can I get you something to drink?

B : Just a cup of coffee, <u>please</u>.

ex. A : Would you like it medium or well-done?

B : medium, <u>please</u>.

Writing Spot

Writing Tips

Countable Nouns	VS	Uncountable Nouns
I eat an apple every day.		I eat bread every day.
I like apples.		I like bread.

You <u>can</u> use <u>a / an</u> with singular countable nouns.

You <u>cannot</u> normally use <u>a / an</u> with uncountable nouns.

ex. There are seven <u>days</u> in a week.

Outside the movie theater there was <u>a line</u> of people waiting to see the movie.

There were very few <u>people</u> in the stores today.

Do It Yourself

Write down the sentences using the following words.

1 there / be / many / mistake / in book

_____.

2 there / be / fax service

_____.

3 there / be / TV and VCR / in room

_____.

4 there / be / 24-hour room service

_____.

5 there / be / three / restaurant / in hotel

_____.

6 there / be / tennis courts / in yard

_____.

7 there / be / people / in auditorium

_____.

3

At the airport:

Checking-in

Building Vocabulary

Match the words with the same meaning.

1. check in •   • ⓐ lay down

2. be off •   • ⓑ a train, bus or plane at a station or an airport
                                   that a passenger can take soon after getting off
                                   another in order to continue their journey

3. carry on •   • ⓒ start

4. mind •   • ⓓ a passage between rows of seats in a church,
                                   theatre, train, etc., or between rows of shelves
                                   in a supermarket

5. put on •   • ⓔ bags, cases, etc. that contain somebody's clothes
                                   and things when they are travelling

6. scale •   • ⓕ bring

7. connection •   • ⓖ a card that you show before you get on a plane
                                   or boat

8. aisle •   • ⓗ to go to a desk in a hotel, an airport, etc; to
                                   leave bags or cases with an official to be put
                                   on a plane or train

9. boarding pass •   • ⓘ an instrument for weighing people or things

10. baggage •   • ⓙ used to ask for permission to do something, or
                                   to ask somebody in a polite way to do something

Reading an Article

Read the time table and answer the following questions.

Pacific Airlines Passenger Briefing

This passenger briefing contains information about our flight itinerary to Boston and Atlanta. Please ask a customer service representative if you need further assistance.

(Thursday 12/23/2009)

Depart	**PHILADELPHIA, PA**	PHILADELPHIA INTL	08:00a.m.
Arrive	**BOSTON, MA**	BOSTON SKY HARBOR INTL	09:53a.m.

Flight Time   00:53   Time Change : Add 1 hour(s)

Catering Info : Light breakfast including danish, fruit and fresh orange juice

---

(Thursday 12/23/2009)

Depart	**BOSTON, MA**	BOSTON SKY HARBOR INTL	10:45a.m.
Arrive	**ATLANTA, GA**	ATLANTA INTL	12:06p.m.

Flight Time   01:15   No Time Change

Special Notes : Transportation from Atlanta Airport to your meeting will be
provided by K&R Limo. Service 304-233-3558

(Friday 12/24/2009)

Depart	**ATLANTA, GA**	ATLANTA INTL	01:00p.m.
Arrive	**BOSTON, MA**	BOSTON SKY HARBOR INTL	02:15p.m.

Flight Time   01:21   No Time Change

Catering Info : Sandwich tray, fresh fruit and light dessert

| Depart | BOSTON, MA | BOSTON SKY HARBOR INTL | 03:00p.m. |
| Arrive | PHILADELPHIA, PA | PHILADELPHIA INTL | 02:53p.m. |

Flight Time   00:55   Time Change : lose 1 hour(s)

1 What is this information related to?

(a) A traveler's itinerary   (b) A train schedule

(c) A flight plan   (d) A pilot's directions

2 What is this passenger's final destination on Thursday?

(a) Philadelphia   (b) Boston

(c) Atlanta   (d) Sky Harbor

3 How much time will be spent flying on the return trip?

(a) 1 hour and 15 minutes   (b) 55 minutes

(c) 1 hour and 10 minutes   (d) 2 hours and 10 minutes

Grammar Tips

Present continuous (be + ing) with a future meaning.

I'm doing some business in New York.

I'm meeting up with my husband in San Francisco for a vacation.

ex. A : What **are you doing** on Monday afternoon?

B : **I'm going** to the library.

ex. A : What time **is** Ted **arriving** tomorrow?

B : At 2:00. **I'm meeting** him at the terminal.

* *Will* is used when you decide to do something at the time of speaking.

ex. Oh, I left the window closed. **I'll** go and open it.

ex. A : What would you like to eat?

    B : <u>I'll</u> have some cheese burger, please.

ex. A : Did you call Pierre?

    B : Oh sorry, I forgot. <u>I'll call</u> him right now.

Which is correct? Choose the correct one.

1 I can't meet you next Saturday morning. <u>I'm playing / I'll play</u> tennis.

2 A : I need some money.

   B : OK, <u>I'm lending / I'll lend</u> you some. How much do you need?

3 <u>I'm throwing / I'll throw</u> a party next Wednesday. I hope you can come.

4 A : <u>Are you doing / Will you do</u> anything Thursday evening?

   B : No, I'm free. Why?

5 I'm too tired to walk home. I think <u>I'm taking / I'll take</u> a taxi.

Listening Spot

Listen to a Conversation

Try to complete the conversation with expressions from the chart below. Then listen and check your answers.

Staff : Good afternoon, ma'am. May I help you?

Alicia : Good afternoon. **1**_____ I'm off to New York.

Staff : May I have your ticket and passport, please?

Alicia : Here you are.

Staff : **2**_____

Alicia : Two. This one to check in and a small one to carry on.

Staff : **3**_____

Alicia : 4_____

Staff : Thank you, ma'am. Your ticket has a further connection to San Francisco and then a return connection from there.

Alicia : Yes, I'm doing some business in New York and I'm meeting up with my husband in San Francisco for a vacation.

Staff : 5_____

Alicia : Aisle side, please.

Staff : Here are your ticket, passport, boarding pass and baggage claim tags. Have a nice flight.

Alicia : Thank you very much.

No, not at all.

Which seat would you prefer, by the window or the aisle?

How many bags do you have?

Would you mind putting your suitcases on the scale?

I'd like to check in.

Listening Tips

There are many silent letters in English words. Look at the following words.

aisle	building	fought	island	knee
knife	knight	knit	white	window

Listen and cross out the silent letter in the following words.

1 answer

2 buy

3 Christmas

4 could

5 daughter

6 eight

7 hour

8 know

9 listen

10 night

11 walk

12 write

Listen the following each conversation and choose the answer.

1 What does the woman plan to do?

(a) Begin a new job   (b) Go to San Diego

(c) Celebrate a birthday   (d) Meet a friend arriving from abroad

2 What is the man doing?

(a) Take a flight   (b) Give his passport

(c) Sell the tickets   (d) Assign a seat

3–5 What should a caller do if a caller need information on tours in Asia?

(a) Press 1   (b) Press 2

(c) Press 3   (d) Press 4

What number will provide information on fare?

(a) 1   (b) 2

(c) 3   (d) 4

What should a caller do if a line is engaged?

(a) Press 3   (b) Press 4

(c) Hang up and call again   (d) Press # and hold

Speaking Spot   Role-play

Would you mind putting your suitcases on the scale?

  No, not at all.

  Of course not.

○———

Would you like a round-trip ticket, ma'am?

Yes.

Of course.

Sure, why not?

Certainly.

○———

Would you mind opening your handbag, ma'am?

Would you mind turning on the air conditioner?

Would you mind putting out your cigarette, please?

Would you mind closing your tray table?

Would you mind if I take these seats?

Do you mind if I smoke in here?

○———

Would you please open your suitcase?

Would you please close the window shade?

Would you please fill out this form?

Would you please show me your boarding pass, sir?

Would you sign here please?

Would you join us for the Saturday's picnic?

Conversation Tips

"Here you are" is often used when you pass somebody something. "Here it is" has the same meaning as "Here you are."

A : May I have your ticket and passport, please?

B : Here you are.

ex. A : Pass me the salt and pepper.

B : Here you are.

ex. A : May I see your boarding pass, sir?

     B : Here it is.

Writing Tips

After <u>mind</u>, <u>enjoy</u>, and <u>finish</u>, we use -ing.

Here are some more verbs and phrases that are followed by -ing.

avoid, deny, consider, admit, suggest, miss, quit, delay, postpone

go on, keep (on), put off, give up

ex. Would you **mind** <u>putting</u> your suitcases on the scale?

    I **enjoy** <u>listening</u> to pop music.

    Sorry to **keep** <u>you waiting</u>.

Do It Yourself

Write down the sentences using the following words.

1 She / give up / try / find cell phone

_____.

2 Although / Dave / 65 years old / he / want / go on / work

_____.

3 He / try / avoid / answer the phone

_____.

4 She / give up / apply / job / yesterday

_____.

5 Have / you / finish / project

_____.

6 He / consider / quit / smoke / now

_____.

7 Boy / deny / steal / toy / department store

_____.

On board

Taking off

Building Vocabulary

Match the words with the same meaning.

1. seat number   •

    • ⓐ one of the separate sections that something such as a piece of furniture or equipment has for keeping things in

2. briefcase   •

    • ⓑ to sit or lie in a relaxed way, with your body leaning backwards

3. overhead   •

    • ⓒ to close or join together the two parts of something; to become closed or joined together

4. compartment   •

    • ⓓ a number that notifies someone of his or her seat

5. take off   •

    • ⓔ a mark used to represent something

6. shortly   •

    • ⓕ to leave the ground and begin to fly

7. fasten   •

    • ⓖ a belt that is attached to the seat in a car or a plane and that you fasten around yourself so that you are not thrown out of the seat if there is an accident

8. seat belt   •

    • ⓗ a flat case used for carrying papers and documents

9. recline   •

    • ⓘ above your head; raised above the ground

10. sign   •

    • ⓙ soon

Read the article and answer the following questions.

Do you often take domestic flights? Collecting air miles, but still not getting anywhere? If you think it takes too long to earn free flights with other frequent flyer programs, you are not alone. Why don't you join the club? The Western Airlines Flight Club. We may not be the most famous, but we can promise you we are one of the best. The Western Airlines Flight Club gets you on free flights faster because we reward you for the number of trips you take, not how many miles you fly. For anyone who takes mostly domestic flights, it's a great way to earn a free flight. Join our club by taking 8 round trips (2 one ways = 1 round trip) within 12 consecutive months on Western Airlines*. Before boarding each flight, have our Customer Service Agent stamp your application. Once you've received 16 stamps, mail in your application and we'll send you a plastic embossed membership card which you will use to receive credit on all future flights, a free round-trip ticket to anywhere in the continental US, and a free drink coupon book. Remember, credit must be obtained prior to flight. Unfortunately, we cannot credit passengers for past flights.

Call 1-800-243-7878 for an application form or download our printable form from our website at www.western.flightclub.co.uk Get started now!

A full list of conditions may be viewed on our website. The number of free flights that can be taken within a 12-month period by an individual is limited to a maximum of four. Stamps are not trasferable.

1 Which of the following is NOT required in order to qualify for a free flight?

(a) Applications must be stamped prior to boarding every flight.

(b) Passengers must fly once a month for 12 months.

(c) Passengers must get 16 stamps.

(d) Applications must be mailed in when they have 16 stamps.

2 What is different about this frequent flyer program?

(a) 2 one-way trips are the same as a roundtrip.

(b) You get a free drink coupon booklet with your first free flight.

(c) The rewards are fast, and you get to join a club.

(d) It doesn't matter how far you fly.

3 How many free flights can a passenger take in one year?

(a) As many as they quality for   (b) A maximum of 12

(c) A maximum of 4   (d) One

4 How can customers obtain an application form?

(a) By flying with Western Airlines

(b) By calling a special phone line or downloading the form

(c) By sending a fax to Western Airlines

(d) By attending a special seminar

Grammar Tips

(1) 〈Will be + ing〉: Something is in the middle of action in the future.

    ex. Don't call me between 6 and 7a.m. We'll be swimming in the pool.

    ex. Tomorrow at 10a.m., he will be taking a TOEIC test.

(2) 〈Will have + p.p〉: Something will already be completed before a time in the future.

    ex. Next year we will have been married for 10 years.

    ex. By the time he wake up, his mother will already have gone to work.

Read and complete the sentences.

1 I _____ at my office until 7, so please contact me then. (stay)

2 Tomorrow evening we _____ tennis. (play)

3 Call on me after 9. We _____ dinner by then. (finish)

4 By the end of bike trip, Nancy _____ more than 3,000 miles. (travel)

5 I am afraid I won't make. I _____ on Saturday morning. (work)

Listening Spot

Listen to a Conversation

Try to complete the conversation with expressions from the chart below. Then listen and check your answers.

Flight Attendant : Good afternoon, ma'am. **1**_____

Alicia : Uh, twenty-nine K.

Flight Attendant : That's on the right side of the airplane. It's by the window. Please step this way, ma'am.

Alicia : Thank you. **2**_____

Flight Attendant : You may put your briefcase in this overhead compartment.

Alicia : Thank you.

Flight Attendant : **3**_____ Would you fasten your seat belt, please?

Alicia : Sure. **4**_____

Flight Attendant : I'm sorry, but not right now. You can recline it when the 'Fasten Seat Belt' sign is turned off after takeoff.

Alicia : Oh, I see. Thank you very much.

Flight Attendant : You're welcome. **5**_____

May I recline my seat?

We'll be taking off shortly.

What's your seat number?

Where can I put my briefcase?

Question words (who, when, where, what, why) can sound confusing in natural speech.

ex. **What's** your seat number?

Where can I put my briefcase?

Listen and put a check(✓) next to the word you hear.

1 ☐ Where
  ☐ Why

2 ☐ When
  ☐ Where

3 ☐ What
  ☐ Who

4 ☐ What
  ☐ Who

5 ☐ What
  ☐ When

6 ☐ Where
  ☐ When

7 ☐ Why
  ☐ Where

8 ☐ Who
  ☐ Where

Further
Listening

Listen the following each conversation and choose the answer.

1 Why is the man anxious for the plane to land?

(a) He does not feel well.

(b) He does not like to fly.

(c) He is late for a meeting.

(d) He has another plane to catch.

2 Where does the conversation take place?

(a) In an apartment

(b) On an airplane

(c) On a ship   (d) In a terminal

3-5 What is the woman's job?

(a) Bank teller   (b) Hotel receptionist

(c) Airport check-in desk clerk (d) Travel agent

How many bags does the man want to keep with him?

(a) All of them   (b) Three of them

(c) None of them   (d) Half of them

What is the man going to do?

(a) Complain to the woman's supervisor

(b) Take a later flight

(c) Pay for excess baggage

(d) Put all his important items together

Role-play

Q : May I recline my seat?

A : You can recline it when the 'Fasten Seat Belt' signs are out after take-off.

Q : Where can I put my briefcase?

A : You may put your briefcase in this overhead compartment.

○————

Can I get you something to drink?

Can I make a copy of this form?

Can I see last month's sales figures?

Can I get an upgrade to business class?

May I see your passport?

May I speak to Mr. Johnson?

May I be of assistance?

Conversation Tips

"Could" is more polite expression than "Can". However, these may be used with no difference.

A : Can I have a cheese sandwich, please?

B : Yes, of course. That's $4.00.

A : Could I have a glass of water, please?

B : Sure. Here you are.

Complete these requests with <u>Can / Could I... ?</u> or <u>Can / Could you... ?</u>

1 _____ tell me the time, please?

2 _____ take me to school?

3 _____ see the menu, please?

4 _____ lend me some money, please?

5 _____ help me with my homework, please?

6 _____ borrow your dictionary, please?

Writing Spot

Conversation Tips

To talk about future actions that have already been planned or decided on, it is polite to use the future continuous tense: ⟨be + ing⟩

ex. We'll be taking off shortly.

Will you be dining at the restaurant?

I will be meeting my husband.

Do It Yourself

Write down the sentences with the future continuous tense using the following words.

1 I / pay / bill / Visa card

_____.

2 She / stay / two nights

_____.

3 I / use / cell phone / daily

_____.

4 I / meet / co-workers / for dinner

_____.

5 He / need / briefcase / right now

_____.

6 I / pay / cash

_____.

7 We / need / day care / tomorrow afternoon

_____.

Unit

5

On board:

Inflight Service

Building Vocabulary

Match the words with the same meaning.

1. serve • • ⓐ the food that is eaten at a meal

2. kind • • ⓑ in addition to somebody[something]

3. meal • • ⓒ a large sea fish that is used for food

4. beef • • ⓓ a glass or bottle of water

5. tuna • • ⓔ right now

6. still • • ⓕ (of a drink) containing bubbles of gas

7. sparkling • • ⓖ a group of people or things that are the same
in some way; a particular variety of type

8. besides • • ⓗ to give somebody food or drink, for example
at restaurant or during a meal

9. mineral water • • ⓘ meat that comes from a cow

10. right away • • ⓙ (of a drink) not containing bubbles of gas

Reading an Article

Read the article and answer the following questions.

How much money do fliers leave behind on airlines? One international carrier took in $75,000 last year, which it donated to charities. That's an average of $18 a passenger. If that figure holds true for all 320 million people who fly on the hundreds of international airlines, it amounts to $58 million per year.

Much less is found on domestic U.S. flights. A cleaning crew in Chicago reported finding less than $10 per flight. An executive of one international airline suggested that on international flights passengers disposed of unwanted coins from the countries they were departing by leaving the coins in their seats or in the seat pockets in front of them.

1 Which is the best headline for this article?

(a) "Saving Money on International Travel"

(b) "The Changing Face of Air Travel"

(c) "How to Hold on to Your Money"

(d) "Loose Change Found on Planes"

2 What is the figure of $58 million mentioned in the first paragraph based on?

(a) Data from hundreds of airlines

(b) Interviews with numerous cleaning crews

(c) Information provided by one airline

(d) Estimates made by airline executives

3 What explanation is offered for the greater amount of money left on international flights than on U.S. domestic flights?

(a) International passengers discard unwanted coins.

(b) U.S. cleaning crews are keeping the money.

(c) International airlines are more interested in charity.

(d) U.S. passengers carry less change.

Grammar Tips

In general, we use <u>some</u> in positive sentences and any in negative and question sentences.

(1) Affirmative

ex. I want to have some mineral water.

(2) Negative

ex. We don't have any Evian.

(3) Question

ex. Do you want any?

We often use <u>any</u> after *If*.

ex. Let me know if you ever need <u>any</u> help.

We also use <u>any</u> with the meaning "*it doesn't matter which*."

ex. Take <u>any</u> book you like.

Complete the sentences with some or any.

1 If you have _____ money with you, please lend me.

2 Would you have _____ coffee, please?

3 In our classroom there are _____ books on the floor.

4 There aren't _____ plants.

5 Are there _____ Chinese students in your class?

6 There aren't _____ Spanish students.

7 We have _____ pencils in the cabinet.

8 There aren't _____ pens in my bag.

Listen to a Conversation

Try to complete the conversation with expressions from the chart below. Then listen and check your answers.

Flight Attendant : Excuse me, ma'am. We're going to serve your dinner now.

1_____

Cecilia : Sure. 2_____

Flight Attendant : We have beef, fish and chicken.

Cecilia : 3_____

Flight Attendant : It's tuna.

Cecilia : Chicken, please.

Flight Attendant : Anything to drink?

Cecilia : Yes. Water, please.

Flight Attendant : 4_____

Cecilia : Evian, please.

Flight Attendant : I'm sorry, but we don't have any Evian.

5_____

Cecilia : Well, I want to have some mineral water.

Flight Attendant : Here you are. If you need some more water, please let me know right away.

Cecilia : Thank you. I'll do that.

Any other water besides Evian?

What kinds of meals do you have today?

What kind of water would you like still or sparkling?

What's the fish?

Would you lower your tray table?

Listening Tips

What's the difference between the sentences?

ex. **There are <u>two</u> magazines.**

ex. **There are <u>some</u> magazines.**

When do we say <u>some</u>? When do you say any?

ex. **There are <u>some</u> cups.**

ex. **There aren't <u>any</u> glasses.**

ex. **Are there <u>any</u> spoons?**

Listen and put a check(✓) next to the sentence you hear.

1 □ There aren't some sandwiches.

  □ There aren't any sandwiches.

2 □ Do you have some good dictionary?

  □ Do you have a good dictionary?

3 □ I have some photos of my dog.

  □ I have any photos of my dog.

4 □ I have lot of books.

  □ I have a lot of books.

5 □ How many students are there in this class?

  □ How many of students are there in this class?

6 □ Next my house there's a park.

  □ Next to my house there's a park.

Listen the following each conversation and choose the answer.

1 Where are they?

(a) At a coffee shop   (b) On an airplane

(c) At the airport   (d) At a restaurant

2 What is the man doing?

(a) Serving breakfast   (b) Shopping for groceries

(c) Ordering coffee   (d) Talking to a friend

3 What does the speaker want?

(a) Somewhere to sit   (b) Something to eat

(c) Something to drink   (d) Something to eat with

4−5 Who is the speaker?

(a) A flight attendant   (b) A pilot

(c) A cabin attendant   (d) A conductor

When will the plane be landing?

(a) In a few minutes   (b) In twenty -five minutes

(c) In fourteen hours   (d) In ten hours

Speaking Spot
Role-play

<u>**What kinds of meals**</u> do you have today?

We have beef, fish and chicken.

<u>What kind of water</u> do you want, still or sparkling?

Evian, please.

○————

<u>What kinds of people</u> will be at the party?

○————

<u>What kind of skirt</u> are you looking for?

<u>What kind of cabinet </u>are you looking for?

<u>What kind of work</u> do you do?

Conversation Tips

In question sentences, we may often omit 〈Auxiliary verb + Subject (+ Verb)〉.

<u>Anything</u> to drink? → <u>Do you want anything</u> to drink?

→ <u>Would you like anything</u> to drink?

ex. <u>Want</u> to get in shape? → <u>Do you want</u> to get in shape?

ex. <u>Need</u> to lose weight? → <u>Do you need</u> to lose weight?

ex. <u>Just want</u> to be fitter? → <u>Do you just want</u> to be fitter?

ex. <u>Stuck</u> at your desk? → <u>Have you stuck</u> at your desk?

Writing Spot

Writing Tips

(1) In a service-providing context, when you are unable to give customers what they want, it is polite to <u>express regret</u> and then <u>make a suggestion</u> of what you can offer.

(2) It helps to stress 'don't' and 'do' as in the sentences below.

(3) Notice that in the negative structure, 'any' is used before the noun, while in the positive part of the sentence, 'some' is used before the noun.

ex. I'm sorry, but we don't have any Evian.

ex. I'm sorry, we don't have any imported wine, but we do have some good local wine.

Do It Yourself

Write down the sentences using the following words.

1 sorry / kiwi juice / mango juice

→ I'm sorry, we don't have any kiwi juice, but we do have some mango juice.

2 sorry / cheese / nuts

_____.

3 sorry / tables on the terrace / tables inside the restaurant

_____.

4 sorry / decaffeinated coffee / regular coffee

_____.

5 sorry / roast chicken / roast beef

_____.

6 sorry / white wine / red wine

_____.

7 sorry / ice cream / whipping cream

_____.

6

On arrival·

Passing through Immigration

Building Vocabulary

Match the words with the same meaning.

1. passport •
2. There you go •
3. purpose •
4. business •
5. import •
6. export •
7. company •
8. stay •
9. prohibited •
10. item •

• ⓐ the activity of making, buying, selling or supplying goods or services for money

• ⓑ not permitted; not allowed

• ⓒ the act of bringing a product or service into one country from another

• ⓓ one thing on a list of things to buy, do, talk about, etc.

• ⓔ the selling and transporting of goods to another country

• ⓕ to live in a place temporarily as a guest or visitor

• ⓖ an official document that identifies you as a citizen of a particular country, and that you may have to show when you enter or leave a country

• ⓗ Here it is.

• ⓘ a business organization that makes money by producing or selling goods or services

• ⓙ the intention, aim or function of something; the thing that something is supposed to achieve

Reading an Article

Read the article and answer the following questions.

Airport Expansion in the Works

FORT REGINALD--The Fort Reginald Ministry of Transportation is currently finalizing plans to expand Mirabel International Airport. According to sources, a minimum of 142 million Euro, more than half coming from overseas investment, is to be earmarked for the project. The Ministry cites the steady increase in air traffic and the deregulation of air transport as the major factors that have led to the elaboration of a project for the expansion and modernization of the current airport.

The main feature of the project will be a major new addition to the terminal, to be designed by the architect Santiago Cervantes. This will expand the total size of the air terminal to cover an area of 25,000 square meters, including five additional gates, and experts estimate it will be capable to handle 2.5 million passengers per year. The groundbreaking ceremony is slated for early this September, and construction is expected to be completed in about 18 months.

1 Where will the largest portion of the funding for the expansion come from?

(a) Mirabel International Airport Authority

(b) Fort Reginald Ministry of Transportation

(c) Passengers

(d) Foreign investors

2 What is NOT part of the proposed plan for the airport?

(a) The demolition of the existing terminal

(b) An investment of more than 142 million Euros

(c) Building more gates to handle more passengers

(d) A new addition designed by a famous architect

Grammar Tips

There are many adjectives ending in ⟨-ing⟩ and ⟨-ed⟩: for example, exciting and excited.

(1) Adjectives with the form of ⟨-ing⟩

 ex. The game was **exciting**.

(2) Adjectives with the form of ⟨-ed⟩

 ex. I was **excited** at the game.

 ex. Do you have any **prohibited** items?

Complete the sentence with the correct form of the verb.

1 He lay down _____ (exhaust).

2 I am sorry to have kept you _____ (wait) so long.

3 She had her photograph _____ (take).

4 There are _____ (burn) candles on the cake.

5 Look at the girl _____ (sing) an English song.

6 The _____ (light) Christmas tree is very beautiful.

7 He gave me a watch _____ (make) in Korea.

8 A boy sat _____ (write) something on the ground.

9 We find _____ (fall) leaves here and there in autumn.

10 I want the film _____ (develop) and _____ (print).

Listen to a Conversation

Try to complete the conversation with expressions from the chart below. Then listen and check your answers.

Immigration Officer : Could I see your passport, please?

Jakob : Yes, 1_____

Immigration Officer : From Taiwan? What's the purpose of your trip?

Jakob : 2_____

Immigration Officer : Excuse me, but what kind of business?

Jakob : 3_____ We do some business with U.S. companies.

Immigration Officer : 4_____

Jakob : About two weeks.

Immigration Officer : 5_____

Jakob : No, I don't.

Immigration Officer : Okay. That's all. Welcome to the United States, and enjoy your stay.

Jakob : Thank you.

Do you have any prohibited items?

I'm doing import and export business.

How long are you staying in the United States?

On business

there you go.

The ⟨-ed⟩ ending of regular verbs has three different pronunciations. Look at the verbs and how each verb is pronounced.

/t/	/d/	/id/
finished	lived	prohibited
liked	learned	started
cooked	cleaned	visited

Listen to the sentences and check the box including the verbs you hear.

	1	2	3	4	5	6	7
/t/							
/d/							
/id/							

Further
Listening

Listen the following each conversation and choose the answer.

1–3 Where are they?

(a) In a coffee shop   (b) In a plane

(c) In a clothing shop   (d) In a beauty shop

What does the woman mean?

(a) There is no more water.   (b) The man should stay quiet.

(c) She can't serve water now.   (d) The route has be changed.

When will the man get served what he wants?

(a) Twenty minutes later   (b) Five minutes later

(c) Right now   (d) Never

4-6 Where is this conversation taking place?

(a) On the bus   (b) At the airport

(c) In the office   (d) At the library

Why is the man visiting Vancouver?

(a) For a wedding   (b) For business

(c) For pleasure   (d) For business and pleasure

How long will the man stay in Vancouver?

(a) One week   (b) Three days

(c) Six days   (d) One month

Role-play

Excuse me, but what kind of business?

  I'm doing import and export business.

  We do some business with U.S. companies.

○———

What are you planning to do during the vacation?

What are you planning to do during the summer?

What are you planning to do during the holiday?

○———

I'm doing some swimming.

I'm doing some sightseeing.

I'm doing some studying.

I'm doing some homework.

"That's all" is used when you are stating. . .

(1) There is nothing more that can be said about something

(2) Something is completely finished.

A : Do you have any prohibited items?

B : No, I don't.

A : Okay. <u>That's all</u>.

ex. That's all.

    = That's all there is to it.

    = That's all she wrote.

ex. That's all for today.

ex. That' all I know.

ex. That's all there is to say.

ex. That's all you know.

Writing Spot

Writing Tips

(1) The auxiliary verbs 'could' and 'can' are often used to ask other people to do things.

(2) 'Could' is more formal than 'can'.

(3) Requests with 'could' are more polite when they are followed by 'please'.

ex. <u>Could[Can]</u> I see your passport, please?

<u>Could[Can]</u> I have your name, please?

<u>Could[Can]</u> I have your credit card, please?

ex. <u>Could[Can]</u> you spell your last name, please?

<u>Could[Can]</u> you tell me your room number, please?

<u>Could[Can]</u> you sign here, please?

<u>Could[Can]</u> you repeat that, please?

Do It Yourself

Write down the sentences using the following words.

1 have / your room key

_____.

2 write / your address

_____.

3 fill out / this form

_____.

4 wait / here

_____.

5 sign / on the bottom line

_____.

6 wait / over there

_____.

Unit

7

On arrival:

Baggage Claim

Building Vocabulary

Match the words with the same meaning.

1. arrive • • ⓐ to return, especially to your home

2. carousel • • ⓑ a moving belt from which you collect your bags at an airport

3. pick up • • ⓒ to receive a letter, email, phone call, etc. from somebody

4. lost • • ⓓ to get to a place, especially at the end of a journey

5. describe • • ⓔ material made by removing the hair or fur from animal skins and preserving the skins using special processes

6. leather • • ⓕ to say what somebody[something] is like

7. shoulder strap • • ⓖ to take hold of somebody[something] and lift them[it] up

8. fill out • • ⓗ to complete a form, ect. by writing information on it

9. get back • • ⓘ that cannot be found or brought back

10. hear from • • ⓙ a long strip of cloth, leather, ect. that is attached to a bag so that you can carry it over your shoulder

Read the notice and answer the following questions.

Thank you for choosing E-Travel. Please keep in mind the following information before you embark on your journey:

1. **Check-in** : When flying domestically, please make sure that you arrive at the airport a minimum of 1 hour before your flight departure time. When flying internationally, we advise you to check in at least 2 hours before the departure time. Please note that if you check in late, you may not be permitted to board the plane.

2. **Overbooking** : Flight can be overbooked. If you are denied boarding, you will be given a compensatory payment in most cases. Please check the rules related to denied boarding and ask any ticket counter agent for the relevant application forms for compensatory payment.

3. **Baggage insurance** : The insurance airlines provide in relation to last or damaged luggage has a very narrow coverage. Also, damages from cancellation, accident, illness or stolen or damaged property may not be sufficiently covered by your own personal insurance. Although the chance of such damage occurring to you is very low statistically, we strongly recommend you to purchase your own additional insurance. This additional insurance may not be cheap, but it is often worthwhile to have. Please check with us to find a list of insurance companies. We strongly recommend you contacting one of these insurance companies to protect yourself.

4. **Prepaid tickets** : If you or someone else has requested a prepaid airline ticket, you can collect the prepaid ticket at the airline ticket counter. Just don't forget to present a valid piece of identification to pick it up. Be aware that most airlines will ask you for a non-refundable service fee before you pick up the ticket. The passenger whose name appears on the reservation will ultimately be responsible for this fee. Please understand that this additional service fee is imposed by the airlines.

1 If a passenger cannot board an overbooked flight, what should they do?

  (a) Call the travel agency right away

  (b) Call a lawyer

  (c) Demand a refund at the airline passenger service counter

  (d) Fill out an application for compensation at the ticket counter

2 According to the travel agency, why is the purchase of additional insurance recommended?

  (a) The insurance airlines provide is often not enough.

  (b) The possibility of damage occurring to one's belongs is very high.

  (c) Buying an additional insurance policy is very cheap.

  (d) Additional insurance protects against every possible scenario, no matter how expensive it is.

3 When someone else purchases a ticket in advance, how can it be picked up?

  (a) By having it delivered by express courier

  (b) By visiting the travel agency

  (c) By asking the flight attendants for help

  (d) By paying a service fee at the ticket counter

Grammar Tips

Present Perfect Simple VS Simple Past

(1) **Present perfect simple : When we talk about a period of time that continues from the past until now**

  ex. I've just arrived from Air Canada.

  ex. Have you ever eaten frog's leg?

(2) **Simple past : When you talk about a finished time**

  ex. What flight were you on?

  ex. We bought our house in 2001.

Sandra is being interviewed. Write questions and answers using the information given. Use the simple past or present perfect simple.

Interviewer : Where were you born, Sandra?

Sandra : I was born in a small town outside of Caracas, Venezuela.

Interviewer : Really? **1**_____?

(how long ago / you move / United States)

Sandra : **2**_____.

(I be here / for 15 years)

Interviewer : **3**_____?

(you go / Venezuela / last year)

Sandra : No, **4**_____.

(I not go / Venezuela / since 1997)

Listening Spot Listen to a Conversation

Try to complete the conversation with expressions from the chart below. Then listen and check your answers.

George : I've just arrived from Air Canada, but my luggage doesn't seem to be here.

Officer : **1**_____

George : Air Canada flight 705.

Officer : Right, **2**_____

George : Yes, I waited there for about an hour. All the other passengers picked up their bags, but mine wasn't there.

Officer : One lost bag. **3**_____

George : Yes, a brown one.

Officer : Can you describe it, please?

George : 4_____

Officer : Could you fill out this form? We'll do our best to get it back, sir.

George : Thank you very much.

Officer : 5_____ Then we'll call you there as soon as we have some information.

George : Okay. I hope to hear from you soon.

It's a brown leather bag with a shoulder strap.

Is it a suitcase?

Tell me which hotel you're staying at.

that's Carousel 3, isn't it?

What flight were you on?

Listening Tips

Compare the pronunciation _can_ with _can't_.

(1) _ex._ I can speak Spanish. = /kən/

(2) _ex._ Yes, I can. = /kæn/

(3) _ex._ No, I can't. = /kænt/

Listen and complete the sentences with can or can't.

1 I _____ speak French, but I _____ speak Korean.

2 He _____ dance, but he _____ sing.

3 They _____ ski, but they _____ swim.

4 We _____ dance and we _____ sing.

Listen and put a check(✓) next to the sentence you hear.

1 □ I don't can use a computer.

□ I can't use a computer.

2 □ Was they at the party?

□ Were they at the party?

3 □ I'm sorry. I can't go to the party.

□ I'm sorry. I no can go to the party.

4 □ She was no at home.

□ She wasn't at home.

5 □ He could play chess when he was five.

□ He can play chess when he was five.

6 □ I can to speak English very well.

□ I can speak English very well.

> Further
> Listening

Listen the following each conversation and choose the answer.

1 What are the speakers discussing?

(a) Where to shop

(b) Where to find their bags

(c) How to get out of the city

(d) How to get to the train station

2-4 What are they discussing?

(a) Weather disaster

(b) Change in flight schedule

(c) Opening speech

(d) Change in seminar schedule

What does the man think is the problem?

(a) He is caught in a rainstorm. (b) He can't leave on schedule.

(c) He has a bad cold. (d) He lost his plane ticket.

Who is the woman?

(a) A secretary (b) A News reporter

(c) An airline receptionist (d) A flight attendant

Speaking Spot Role-play

Which hotel are you staying at?

  Tell me which hotel you're staying at.

Which car is the dining car?

  Tell me which car is the dining car.

○————

Where is Mr. Richardson's office?

  Tell me where Mr. Richardson's office is.

Where can I find Mr. Robert?

  Tell me where I can find Mr. Robert.

Where is he?

  Tell me where he is.

Where do I have to go to find the boardroom?

  Tell me where I have to go to find the boardroom.

○————

How far is it to downtown?

Tell me how far it is to downtown.

Conversation Tips

You can use **as . . . as** in positive sentences and questions:

We'll call you there as soon as we have some information.

ex. I'll give you a ring as soon as I get the answer from him.

ex. I'll introduce her to you as soon as she gets to our office.

ex. Please contact us as soon as possible.

ex. Please call me as soon as possible. = Please call me as soon as you can.

ex. I'm going to apply for my vacation time as soon as possible.

ex. I need the information quickly, so please let me know as soon as possible.

ex. Please leave a brief message and I will get back to you as soon as possible.

ex. As soon as she saw him, she began to cry.

Writing Tips

Use tag questions to check information or ask for agreement. Look at the example and the following chart.

ex. **That's Carousel 3, isn't it?**

Tag question : Simple present and simple past	
Affirmative sentence	*Negative sentence*
That's true, <u>isn't it</u>?	That isn't true, <u>is it</u>?
The movie was based on a true story, <u>wasn't it</u>?	The movie wasn't based on a true story, <u>was it</u>?
That sounds like a Hollywood ending, <u>doesn't it</u>?	That doesn't sound like a Hollywood ending, <u>does it</u>?
He gave her half his winnings, <u>didn't he</u>?	He didn't give her half his winnings, <u>did he</u>?

Match the beginnings(1-8) with the tag questions(a-h).

1 She's from London, . .   ⓐ does he?

2 It's a beautiful day, . .   ⓑ was it?

3 You don't like to borrow money, . .   ⓒ isn't it?

4 You aren't from around here, . .   ⓓ do you?

5 They paid for dinner, . .   ⓔ weren't you?

6 Kevin doesn't like spending money, . .   ⓕ are you?

7 The bank wasn't open today, . .   ⓖ isn't she?

8 You were working yesterday, . .   ⓗ didn't they?

Do It Yourself

Complete the conversation with tag questions and short answers.

Interviewer : Welcome, radio listeners. We are talking to Anna Lee, of Boston,

Massachusettes. Ms. Lee, you're Harold's neighbor,

1_____?

Anna   : Yes, **2**_____. And I'm very lucky to be one of

them, too.

Interviewer : He's a very generous man, **3**_____?

Anna   : Yes, **4**_____. He's always been a good neighbor.

Interviewer : But you didn't expect this kind of help from him,

5_____?

Anna   : No, **6**_____. I mean, we didn't know he had

that kind of money in his barn, **7**_____?

On arrival:

Passing through Customs

Building Vocabulary

Match the words with the same meaning.

1. declare • • ⓐ used to make or agree to a suggestion

2. suitcase • • ⓑ shut

3. why not • • ⓒ any alcoholic drink

4. liquor • • ⓓ to estimate how much money will be needed for something or the price that should be charged for something

5. pack • • ⓔ a piece of paper that shows that goods or services have been paid for

6. ginseng • • ⓕ enjoyable, pleasing or attractive

7. cost • • ⓖ a number of things that are wrapped or tied together, especially for carrying

8. receipt • • ⓗ a case with flat sides and a handle, used for carrying clothes, etc. when you are travelling

9. close • • ⓘ a medicine obtained from a plant root that some people believe helps you stay young ad healthy

10. pleasant • • ⓙ to tell customs officers that you are carrying goods on which you should pay tax

Read the article and answer the following questions.

(Center City) The Metro Airport Authority (MAA) announced at a news conference today that it has reached a long-sought agreement with Great Lakes Airways to increase flight service at both local airports. MAA spokesman William Henry James told reporters the airline had agreed to add two new weekly departures for and one new daily arrival from Chicago to its existing City Airport schedule, and that County Airport would see one new daily round trip to Chicago and one more daily departure for Buffalo. Though the starting dates for the new flight service have yet to be formalized, James said that he and Great Lakes representatives had an understanding that all new flights would be on the airline's schedule by the end of November or early December. Making the announcement at city hall this morning, James said that the schedule changes should be especially welcome news for local business travelers, many of whom have criticized the MAA for its inability to persuade airlines serving the area to expand their schedules.

1 According to the information given, which of the following will be the result of the flight schedule changes?

(a) City Airport will be busier than County Airport.

(b) Prices for airline tickets in Center City will decline.

(c) There will be one more daily flight to Buffalo from County Airport.

(d) Criticism of the Metro Airport Authority will cease.

2 When the changes take effect, how many new flights will be departing from County Airport each day?

(a) One   (b) Two

(c) Four   (d) Seven

3 What is true of William Henry James?

(a) He works for the Metro Airport Authority.

(b) His office is at City Airport.

(c) He works for Great Lakes Airlines.

(d) His office is at city hall.

4 What is true of the increase in flight service to the Center City area?

(a) It will begin in January.

(b) It will increase local taxes.

(c) It was desired by local business travelers.

(d) There will be new flights to several cities.

Grammar Tips

a / an + singular countable nouns

a . . . of + uncountable noun

one[a] pack of ginseng tea / four packs of ginseng tea

a[one] bottle of honey / five bottles of honey

a glass[can] of orange juice / seven glasses[cans] of orange juice

a cup of coffee / three cups of coffee

a piece[sheet] of paper / twelve pieces[sheets] of paper

a piece of advice / two pieces of advice

a loaf of bread / six loaves of bread

a drop of water / a hundred drops of water

Read and complete the sentences.

1 Please give me a _____ of chalk.

2 Will you have a _____ of milk?

3 She washed a _____ of socks.

4 She put on a new _____ of clothes.

5 She put two s-_____ of sugar into the cup.

6 He came home with half a dozen _____ of wine.

Listen to a Conversation

Try to complete the conversation with expressions from the chart below. Then listen and check your answers.

Customs officer : 1 _____

Rick : No, I have nothing to declare.

Customs officer : Would you please open your suitcase?

Rick : 2 _____

Customs officer : 3 _____

Rick : Yes, I've one pack of ginseng tea and two bottles of honey. They're all for my parents living in Denver.

Customs officer : 4 _____

Rick : 120 dollars.

Customs officer : 5 _____

Rick : Yes, of course. Here it is.

Customs officer : Okay. You may close your suitcase now. Have a pleasant trip.

Rick : Thank you. Bye.

Do you have a receipt for it?

Sure, why not?

Do you have any cigarettes, liquor or gifts?

How much did it cost?

Do you have anything to declare?

Listening Tips

Look at the prices.

$1.00 one dollar / a dollar

$100 one hundred dollars / a hundred dollars

$120 one hundred and twenty dollars / one hundred twenty dollars

$0.30 / 30¢ thirty cents

$8.50 eight dollars and fifty cents / eight-fifty

Write the prices you hear. Practice saying them.

1 _____

2 _____

3 _____

4 _____

5 _____

6 _____

Further
Listening

Listen the following each conversation and choose the answer.

1 Where is this conversation taking place?

   (a) At a restaurant   (b) In Boston

   (c) At an airline desk   (d) At a theater

2 Why did the woman NOT go farther?

    (a) Her son asked her not to.

    (b) Her plane had already left.

    (c) She did not have a boarding pass.

    (d) She was carrying too much luggage.

3 How long will the woman's flight to London be?

    (a) Eight hours   (b) Nine hours

    (c) Ten hours   (d) Eleven hours

4–5 Where is this announcement being made?

    (a) In an airport   (b) In a department store

    (c) In a souvenir shop   (d) At a craft market

    Which of the following was NOT mentioned?

    (a) Photography equipment   (b) Duty Free Alcohol

    (c) Clothing   (d) Handbags

Further Listening Role-play

How much did it cost?	120 dollars

How much is it?	**Nine dollars and ninety-nine cents.**
How much is a bottle of whiskey?	**Eight dollars**

How much is that sweater?	It's on sale for half price.
How much money will it cost?	It should be fairly cheap.
How much is the electric calculator?	Do you mean the blue one?

"Have a adj. + noun" is used in various situations.

A : You may close your suitcase now. Have a pleasant trip.

B : Thank you. Bye.

ex. A : I am going out with Jane this afternoon.

　　B : Have a good time.

ex. A : I'm so tired that I am going to bed early.

　　B : Have a sound sleep.

ex. A : I've got to go. I am going to concert with my husband tonight.

　　B : Good-bye. Have a nice evening.

Writing Spot

Writing Tips

In conversation, defining relative clauses are often reduced by omitting the relative pronoun and the auxiliary verb.

They're all for my parents (who is[that is]) living in Denver.

ex. Everyone (who is[that is]) going on the scenic flight will have to get up early.

　　Everyone (who is[that is]) going to the desert wears good strong shoes.

Do It Yourself

Make one sentence from two sentences.

1 Look at a boy and his dog. The boy and his dog are running over there.

_____.

2 I was awakened by a bell. The bell was ringing.

_____.

3 Do you know a woman? The woman is talking to Tom.

_____.

4 I have a large bedroom. The bedroom overlooks the garden.

_____.

5 Some of the people can't come. They have been invited to the party.

_____.

6 A receptionist won a lotto. The receptionist works at night.

_____.

7 A waiter passed entrance exams for college. The waiter was serving in the restaurant.

_____.

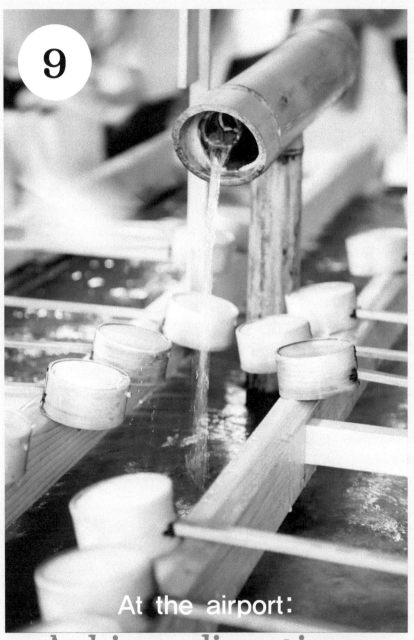

9

At the airport:
Asking directions

Building Vocabulary

Match the words with the same meaning.

1. direction • • ⓐ in or towards the centre of a city, especially its main business area

2. do some shopping • • ⓑ the general position a person or thing moves or points towards

3. department store • • ⓒ a place where trains stop so that passengers can get on and off

4. downtown • • ⓓ a building or set of buildings at an airport where air passengers arrive and leave

5. shuttle • • ⓔ go shopping

6. bus stop • • ⓕ to be close to

7. What about. . . ? • • ⓖ a large shop / store that is divided into several parts, each part selling a different type of goods

8. station • • ⓗ a plane, bus or train that travels regularly between two places

9. isn't far from • • ⓘ Why don't you. . . ?

10. terminal • • ⓙ bus stand

Reading an Article

Read the article and answer the following questions.

The Star, evening edition, Aug. 2
No free meals on Kingfisher Airlines

As of October 1, Kingfisher Airlines will no longer offer complimentary meal service for passengers in economy class. Kingfisher's spokesperson announced yesterday that the airline has decided to stop the free meal service starting on October 1. Snack boxes, however, will be sold to passengers for $7. The menu can be found on Kingfisher Airlines' website: breakfast will consist of an assortment of gourmet cheese and crackers, accompanied by a fresh seasonal fruit mixture and fresh yogurt. For lunch and dinner, passengers can choose from three types of salads with seasonal mixed fruit or three types of sandwich wraps accompanied with a bag of chips. Soft drinks, coffee and tea will still be provided to all passengers at no extra charge.

Recently, an increasing number of airlines have stopped serving free meals in economy class on domestic flight, as they struggle to curb financial losses, especially from high fuel prices. Even major airlines such as United Airlines have discontinued free meals in economy on domestic flights, and even some overseas flights. Several European and Asian airlines are also considering the idea of charging for meals, as they, too, struggle with high fuel prices.

1 What is the topic of the article?

(a) Kingfisher Airlines' financial report

(b) The new meal policy of Kingfisher Airlines

(c) A list of airlines offering the best food

(d) Price comparison between various regional airlines

2 What is suggested about Kingfisher Airlines?

   (a) The airline will reduce its airfares soon.

   (b) It will elect a new CEO.

   (c) It has joined other airlines in attempting to cut losses.

   (d) It treats all passengers equally regardless of where they are sitting on the plane.

3 What is NOT included in the snack box menu?

   (a) Coffee   (b) Cheese

   (c) Salad   (d) Sandwich

Grammar Tips

Using adjectives to compare things

(1) Use ⟨-er⟩ with short(one-syllable) adjectives and ⟨-ier⟩ with two-syllable adjectives that end in ⟨y⟩.

   * large − larger

   * pretty − prettier

(2) Use more with long adjectives (more than one syllable).

   * beautiful − more beautiful

(3) There are many irregular comparative forms.

   * many / much − more

   * few / little − less

   * good / well − better

   ex. The subway takes less time (than the bus).

Read the ads and compare the CD players.

SALE!!!	Special Discount!!!
Electra Compact Disc Player	**Sonic Portable Disc Guy**
3−Disc Changer	Shock Protection
3kg	1kg
35cm × 30cm × 10cm	14cm × 14cm × 3cm
New Model only $159.98	Last year's Model $119.99

1 The Electra is _____ (big) than the Sonic.

2 The Sonic is _____ (expensive).

3 The _____ is _____ (heavy).

4 The _____ is _____ (new).

5 The _____ is _____ (small).

Listening Spot

Listen to a Conversation

Try to complete the conversation with expressions from the chart below. Then listen and check your answers.

Information Officer : What can I do for you, ma'am?

Sharon : 1 _____

I'd like to do some shopping at one of the big department stores.

Information Officer : Most of the big stores are downtown.

Sharon : 2 _____

Information Officer : If you go by bus, it takes about 30 minutes.

Sharon : 3 _____

Information Officer : Sure. Just go right through those doors. The shuttle bus
stop is right outside.

Sharon　　　　　: 4 _____

Information Officer : The subway takes less time and the subway station isn't
far from here, too.

Sharon　　　　　: 5 _____

Information Officer : You go out of the airport terminal, turn right, and it's
a five-minute walk.

Sharon　　　　　: OK, thanks a lot.

Information Officer : It's my pleasure, ma'am.

I need some directions.

Is there a shuttle bus to downtown Vancouver?

How do I get there?

What about going by train?

What's the best way to get there?

Listening Tips

Sometimes prepositions (for example, in, on, at) are not stressed(weak) when
spoken quickly. The following example uses the weak form of at.

ex. I'd like to do some shopping <u>at</u> one of the big department stores.

Listen to the sentences. What preposition does the speaker use? Complete the sentences.

1 We can learn how _____ act.

2 What do you think _____ the baseball club?

3 We can have a lot _____ fun.

4 Do you want _____ join the art club?

5 I'll meet you _____ the park.

6 Can you think _____ anything else?

7 Do you have _____ study tonight?

Further
Listening

Listen the following each conversation and choose the answer.

1 What did the man ask for?

(a) A room   (b) The time

(c) Lighting   (d) Directions

2 When does the shuttle leave for the airport?

(a) Every half hour   (b) Every hour

(c) Every 3 hours   (d) Three times a day

3-5 How long will it take to drive to the university?

(a) Very far   (b) Fifteen miles

(c) Twenty minutes   (d) A long time

Why is the woman surprised?

(a) She thought the university was nearer.

(b) She thought the university was farther.

(c) The university is very beautiful.

(d) The man was very rude to her.

Why does it take so long by bus?

(a) The bus runs once an hour.   (b) The bus route is not direct.

(c) The driver is very slow.   (d) The buses are very old.

Role-play

If you go by bus, it takes about 30 minutes.

○———

If you have a test, you feel this way.

If you study hard but fail, you feel this way.

○———

If you work hard, you'll succeed.

If he is honest, I'll employ him.

If it is rains today, I'll stay at home.

If you call the newspaper, I'll buy the things we need.

If you do that, I'll clean up afterward.

○———

If I go shopping, would you call everyone?

If I get some sandwiches, could you pick up some sandwiches?

Conversation Tips

*** What about going by train?

= How about going by train?

= Let's go by train.

= Why don't you go by train?

= Why don't we go by train?

= How would you like to go by train?

= Would you like to go by train?

ex. How about the next day?

ex. How about Saturday or Sunday?

ex. How about having a drink after work?

ex. How about meeting at the bank machine next to Golden Gate restaurant?

ex. Let's enjoy the day.

ex. Let's try for Thursday morning.

ex. Let's get together during lunch today.

ex. Let's go over the report on last week's sales.

ex. Why don't you give him a call and find out?

ex. Why don't you just go and look at one on the wall?

ex. Why don't you get the receipt from your friend and come back at another time?

ex. Why don't we just walk along the bike path?

ex. Why don't we discuss it with one of the counselors?

ex. Why don't we come by either on Thursday or Friday afternoon?

Writing Spot

Writing Tips

(1) The verb "to take" is often used to describe the time that is needed for an action to be completed. In the following examples, the false subject "it" stands for the trip from the hotel to the city. The usual tense is the simple present.

　　ex. It takes about 30 minutes.

　　ex. The subway takes less time

ex. After a serious accident, it can take some time for the wounds to heal.

(2) **The verb "to spend" is often used to describe the person that uses time for a particular purpose. It is also used to describe giving money to pay for goods, services, etc.**

ex. He spends most of his time working.

ex. He spent the evening wrapping up the Christmas presents.

ex. I've spent all my money already.

Do It Yourself

Write sentences with "take" to express the length of time required for an action using the following words.

1 taxi to airport / fifteen minutes

_____.

2 trip to National Museum / half an hour

_____.

3 it / less time / bicycle

_____.

4 bus / three hours / because / traffic

_____.

5 how long / get there / ?

_____.

6 trip to zoo / one and half an hour

_____.

7 walk / subway station / ten minutes

_____.

Unit

10

At the hotel:

Checking-in

Building Vocabulary

Match the words with the same meaning.

1. reservation •

2. Let me check •

3. try •

4. double room •

5. ocean view •

6. floor •

7. complete •

8. registration card •

9. bellboy •

10. key card •

• ⓐ a bedroom for two people

• ⓑ an attendant in a hotel who performs services such as carrying guests' luggage

• ⓒ to write all the information you are asked for on a form

• ⓓ a certificate that attests to the registering of a person

• ⓔ all the rooms or areas on the same level of a building; a story

• ⓕ a small plastic card that can be used instead of a door key, bearing magnetically encoded data that can be read and processed by an electronic device.

• ⓖ an arrangement for a seat on a plane or train, a room in a hotel, etc. to be kept for you

• ⓗ to use, do or test something in order to see if it is good, suitable, etc.

• ⓘ I'll check it for you.

• ⓙ beautiful scenery of the beach

Reading an Article

Read the article and answer the following questions.

Aqua World Resort Hotel

The most sumptuously furnished and appointed hotel in the country.

- Each suite with a fully equipped kitchen, a formal dining area, and two bathrooms
- Year-round air conditioning
- 7-day maid service
- 24-hour reception / porterage
- Indoor / outdoor swimming pool, tennis and squash courts
- 1.2 hectares of manicured gardens
- World-class restaurants and lounges
- Shopping areas within walking distance

The Lucky Fish : So opulent and yet so friendly. You may decided to spend every moment within its welcoming confines.

1 What is promoted as the most attractive feature of the hotel?

   (a) Its size   (b) Its price

   (c) Its luxury   (d) Its location

2 Why does the hotel say people may not want to venture outside?

   (a) The services are all indoors.

   (b) The hotel is very comfortable.

   (c) The weather is oppressively hot.

   (d) The hotel is in an isolated rural setting.

Writing Tips

*** What's the date today?

(1) We write : 10/14/2010 or October, 14, 2010

(2) We say : "October fourteenth, two thousand ten."

(3) Notice how we say these years:

1900 "Nineteen hundred"   1905 "Nineteen oh five"

1999 "Nineteen ninety-nine"   2001 "Two thousand one"

A. Write the correct word next to the numbers.

fourth	twelfth	sixth	twentieth	second
thirtieth	thirteenth	twenty–first	thirty–first	fifth
seventeenth	tenth	sixteenth	first	third

1 1st _____   **2** 2nd _____   **3** 3rd _____

4 4th _____   **5** 5th _____   **6** 6th _____

7 10th _____   **8** 12th _____   **9** 13th _____

10 16th _____   **11** 17th _____   **12** 20th _____

13 21st _____   **14** 30th _____   **15** 31st _____

B. Practice saying these dates.

1 April 1 _____   **2** March 2 _____

3 September 17 _____   **4** November 19 _____

5 June 23 _____   **6** 2/29/76 _____

7 12/19/83 _____   **8** 10/3/99 _____

9 5/31/2000 _____   **10** 7/15/2004 _____

Listen to a Conversation

Try to complete the conversation with expressions from the chart below. Then listen and check your answers.

Hotel Receptionist : Good evening, sir.

Charles   : Good evening. I want to check in.

Hotel Receptionist : 1 _____

Charles   : Yes, I do. My name is Charles, Santos.

Hotel Receptionist : Let me check . . . I don't have your name on the computer.

Charles   : 2 _____

That's LG Chemistry Company.

Hotel Receptionist : Did you say "LG Chemistry Company?" Ah, yes. I have it here. **3** _____

Charles   : For three night, October 14th to 17th.

Hotel Receptionist : Yes, a double room for three nights with an ocean view. You'll be in Room 702--that's on the fifth floor.

4 _____

Charles   : I'll be paying by credit card.

Hotel Receptionist : OK. I just need you to complete this registration card.

Charles   : Thank you. Uh, sorry, **5** _____

Hotel Receptionist : October 14th, 2010. You're in Room 702. Here is your key card. The bellboy will bring up your luggage. Enjoy your stay.

Charles   : Thank you very much.

How many nights are you staying?

Try my company.

what's the date today?

Do you have a reservation?

How will you be paying, credit card or cash?

Listening Tips

In checking what someone said, use a stronger tone when you are surprised.
Compare the two questions.

ex. Did you say his name is Paul? (checking)

Did you say his name is "**Paul**"? (surprised)

Listen to the questions. Is the speaker checking or surprised?

	1	2	3	4	5	6	7
Checking							
Surprised							

Further
Listening

Listen the following each conversation and choose the answer.

1 Who is the man?

(a) A restaurant owner   (b) A front desk clerk

(c) An airlines agent   (d) A hospital attendant

2 What accommodation can the hotel provide?

(a) Two single rooms   (b) Two double rooms

(c) One single room   (d) One double room

3-5 Where is this conversation taking place?

   (a) At a university   (b) At a hotel

   (c) On the subway   (d) At home

Why will the man leave his room late?

   (a) He will wake up late.   (b) He is expecting a phone call.

   (c) He wants to stay longer.   (d) He lost his room key.

What time will the man probably leave?

   (a) 11:30   (b) 11:00

   (c) 10:30   (d) 10:00

Role-play

A : Do you have a reservation?

B : Yes, I do. My name is Charles, Santos.

A : Let me check. (= I'll check it for you.)

○———

A : I don't have a reservation. But I wonder if there is a room available tonight.

B : Let me check.

○———

A : Someone left this file on the boardroom table. Where is it supposed to go?

B : Let me see.

○———

A : The seventh annual championship of the chess club is on the tenth. Do you
    want to attend, Paul?

B : Let me check my calendar.

Please let me know.

Please let me know if I can help in any way.

Let me call him now.

Let me get the key from my apartment.

Let me call Mr. Smith at Pacific Express right away.

Let me check on the internet to see if there's a center near my place.

Let me go back to the front desk and ask them to call a taxi for us.

Let me get back to my desk and continue to work on my report.

I'll call him and let him know right away.

I'll ask him over lunch today and let you know by one o'clock.

I'm at home right now, so let me know what you think is best.

Conversation Tips

If you don't understand what someone said, repeat what you think you heard as a question. It's a fast way to check for understanding.

A : That's LG Chemistry Company.

B : Did you say "LG Chemistry Company?"

A : The soccer club is the most important thing.

B : Did you say "the soccer club"?

ex. A : Flora, the first question is "what's the most terrible thing about school?"

    B : Did you say "the most terrible thing"?

ex. A : Ruel, here's your question: "What's the most fun thing about school?"

    B : Did you say "the most fun"?

ex. A : I like studying geography.

B : Did you say "geography"?

A : Yeah. I think it's interesting.

Writing Tips

Complete the questions using much or many.

1 How _____ nights are you staying?

2 How _____ people are there in your party?

3 How _____ money do you have in your pocket?

4 How _____ cups of coffee do you drink a day?

5 How _____ gas is there in your car?

6 How _____ apples do you want?

7 How _____ wine do we want?

Do It Yourself

Write down the sentences using the following words.

1 How / (many / much) / books / you / want?

_____.

2 I / don't like / ice cream.

_____.

3 Can / I / have / (some / any) / bread / please?

_____.

4 I / like / sandwich.

_____.

I'm hungry. _____.

5 I / don't have / (many / much) milk / left.

_____.

6 I / like / (some / any) / fruit / please.

_____.

7 How / (many / much) / money / you have?

_____.

8 We / have / (many / much) / homework / today.

_____.

Unit

11

At the hotel restaurant:

Taking orders for food

Building Vocabulary

Match the words with the same meaning.

1. terrace • • ⓐ like (one thing or person) better than another or others

2. prefer • • ⓑ a common freshwater fish that is used for food

3. a bit • • ⓒ to give somebody food or drink, for example at a restaurant or during a meal

4. special • • ⓓ a fungus with a round flat head and short stem.

5. trout • • ⓔ a plant or part of a plant that is eaten as food

6. clam chowder • • ⓕ a little

7. pan-fried • • ⓖ a dish not on the regular menu at a restaurant but served on a particular day

8. serve • • ⓗ a kind of soup with shellfish

9. vegetable • • ⓘ fried in a pan in shallow fat

10. mushroom • • ⓙ a level paved area or platform next to a building; a patio or veranda

Reading an Article

Read the article and answer the following questions.

Les Faires

River Gauche

Appetizers :

Smoked salmon	$4.95
Brie and crackers	$3.15

Entrees :

Beef tips au jus	$14.95
Chicken Kiev	$12.95
Grilled swordfish	$16.95

Includes salad and vegetable

Beverages :

Coffee	$1.50
Tea	$1.50
Soft drinks	$0.75

Desserts :

Ice cream	$1.00
Chocolate cake	$1.50
Fruit w / cream (in season)	$2.50

Tax and tip not included.

1 What is the least expensive item on the Les Faires menu?

   (a) Ice cream   (b) Swordfish

   (c) Soft drinks   (d) Brie and crackers

2 What item is available only at certain times of the year?

   (a) Fish   (b) Salad

   (c) Fruit   (d) Cheese

3 What menu items are NOT charged separately?

   (a) Tax and tip   (b) Coffee and tea

   (c) Bread and butter   (d) Salad and vegetable

Grammar Tips

Compound adjectives : A noun, an adjective or a verb made of two or more words or parts of words, written as one or more words, or joined by a hyphen.

A. Underline the compound adjectives in this paragraph.

My cousin, Oliver, is a well-known musician. He's very good, but he's also very absent-minded. He always keeps a To Do list to remember thing. He has a full-time job and travels a lot. He just bought a brand-new house, but he isn't there much because he's always traveling. He's a well-dressed man; he loves nice clothes. He's left-handed, and he says that's why he's so creative. I don't agree because I'm right-handed, and I'm very creative, too!

B. Fill in the blanks with the adjectives below.

first-class	right-handed	brand-new
good-looking	short-sleeved	full-time

1 We always wear ＿＿＿＿＿＿ shirts in summer.

2 He's very ＿＿＿＿＿＿. He looks like a movie star.

3 I broke my right arm. It's difficult to do things because I'm _____.

4 Morgan just got a _____ job. He only worked ten hours a week before.

5 _____ airplane tickets cost three times more than coach tickets.

6 Old cars are too much trouble. I want to buy a _____ one.

Listening Spot

Listen to a Conversation

Try to complete the conversation with expressions from the chart below. Then listen and check your answers.

Waiter : Good evening. Do you have a reservation?

Steve : No, but I'm staying at this hotel. **1**_____

Waiter : Yes, here we are. Now, there's a table near the window or one out on the terrace. **2**_____

Steve : It's a bit cold today. I think I'll stay inside.

Waiter : Yes, let me show you to your table. . .

Here is the menu. **3**_____

The fish of the day is trout and the soup is clam chowder.

Steve : 4_____

Waiter : Oh, it's very nice. It's pan-fried and served with a herb sauce.

Steve : OK, I'll have the steak.

Waiter : How would you like that cooked?

Steve : Medium rare, thanks. Oh, **5**_____

Waiter : It's served with vegetables and a mushroom sauce.

Steve : That's fine. Can I have two bottles of beer, please?

Waiter : Sure. I'll be right back with your drinks.

Do you have a table for two?

Let me tell you about our specials today.

Which one would you prefer?

what's that served with?

What's the trout like?

Listening Tips

Would like / Do you like . . . ? or I *like / I'd like* can sound confusing in natural speech.

ex. I like to play a guitar.

I'd like to play a guitar.

Listen and put a check(✓) next to the sentence you hear.

1 A : ☐ Would you like a cigarette?

☐ Do you like a cigarette?

B : No, thanks. I don't smoke.

2 A : ☐ Do you like your teacher?

☐ Would you like your teacher?

B : Yes. She's very nice.

3 A : ☐ Do you like a drink?

☐ Would you like a drink?

B : Yes. I'd like a soda, please.

4 A : Can I help you?

B : ☐ Yes. I like a book of stamps, please.

☐ Yes. I'd like a book of stamps, please.

5 A : What sports do you like?

B : ☐ Well, I'd like swimming very much.

☐ Well, I like swimming very much.

6 A : Excuse me, are you ready to order?

B : ☐ Yes. I like a hamburger, please.

☐ Yes. I'd like a hamburger, please.

7 ☐ I like all kinds of fruit.

☐ I'd like some fruit.

8 ☐ I'd like a book by John Bunyan.

☐ I like books by John Bunyan.

9 ☐ I'd like a new bike.

☐ I like riding my bike.

10 ☐ I'd like a cat but not a dog.

☐ I like cats, but I don't like dogs.

Further
Listening

Listen the following each conversation and choose the answer.

1 Where are the speakers?

(a) At home   (b) In a clothing store

(c) In a restaurant   (d) In a library

2 What does the man say he wants to do?

(a) Sit down   (b) Go elsewhere

(c) Buy some tables   (d) See what the restaurant serves

3–5 Which beverage is temporarily unavailable?

(a) Wine   (b) Iced tea

(c) Lemonade   (d) Soda

What does the waitress say about ordering from the dinner menu?

(a) There are fewer choices.   (b) It is more expensive.

(c) She recommends it.   (d) The food will take longer.

How many alcoholic beverages are served?

(a) One   (b) Two

(c) Three   (d) None

Speaking Spot

Role-play

What's the trout like?	Oh, it's very nice.
What's Mexico City like?	It's beautiful.
What's she like?	She's very outgoing.
What's he like?	He's kind of shy.
	She's really smart.
What's his hair like?	It's short and curly.
What's her hair like?	She has long, black hair.
	He's bald.
How are you?	I'm fine.
How is your husband?	He's fine.
How are your children?	They're fine.
How was your party last night?	It was fine until about eleven.

It is important to distinguish between "like" as a verb, such as "Would you like a drink" and "like" as a preposition, such as "What's the trout like?

A : <u>What's</u> the trout <u>like</u>?

B : Oh, it's very nice.

A : <u>How would you like</u> that cooked?

B : Medium rare, thanks.

Practise questions with "What . . . like?" using the following words.

1 what / soup

2 what / weather

3 what / restaurant

4 what / local beer

5 what / beaches

6 what / music

7 what / facilities

Writing Spot

For polite order, the imperative form of the verb "to let" is followed by the direct object "me" and the base verb--the infinitive form of the verb without "to".

128

ex. <u>Let me show</u> you to your table.

ex. <u>Let me tell</u> you about the specials.

ex. <u>Let me take</u> your coat.

Do It Yourself

Write polite offers with "Let me" using the following words.

1 show / menu

_____.

2 give / table / near / window

_____.

3 show / how to use / fax machine

_____.

4 take / to / shopping mall

_____.

5 take / your bags / to / your room

_____.

6 check / air conditioning

_____.

7 read / TV program guide / to you

_____.

Unit

12

On tour:
Sightseeing

Writing Spot

Building Vocabulary

Match the words with the same meaning.

1. pleasant • • ⓐ extremely good; excellent

2. whole • • ⓑ the sport or activity of moving on ice on skates

3. crowded • • ⓒ a street in a town or city

4. fantastic • • ⓓ having good luck

5. avenue • • ⓔ enjoyable, pleasing or attractive

6. Chinatown • • ⓕ to think carefully about the different possibilities that are available and choose one of them

7. suggest • • ⓖ to put forward an idea or a plan for other people to think about

8. ice-skating • • ⓗ the area of a city where many Chinese people live and there are Chinese shops, stores and restaurants

9. decide • • ⓘ full; complete

10. lucky • • ⓙ having a lot of people or too many people

Reading an Article

Read the article and answer the following questions.

The Lakeside Shakespeare Theater

Opening Play Saturday

Join today!

Join by March 4th to receive a free bag

Come to see spectacular City Shakespeare Company's
The Taming of the Shrew

Preview for members only: Thursday, March 10th

Special benefits only for members: Show discounts, members--only nights, and monthly newsletters

2 free tickets to The Taming of the Shrew can be won in the membership lottery

Coming on July 15th and showing all summer: *A Midsummer Night's Dream*

1 When can members first see *The Taming of the Shrew*?

   (a) On February 20   (b) On March 4

   (c) On March 10   (d) On July 15

2 What can be won in a membership lottery?

   (a) Free tickets to a play   (b) A free bag

   (c) Discounts   (d) Special benefits

Present Perfect Simple is 〈have / has + past participle〉. When we use the Present Perfect Simple tense, there is a connection with now. The action in the past has a result now.

ex. I <u>have been</u> to America.

ex. She <u>has been</u> ill since last week.

ex. Have you ever <u>visited</u> Seattle?

Complete the sentence with suitable word form.

1 I began to read the novel last week and _____ (just / finish) it.

2 The boy _____ (be) ill for the past ten days.

3 I _____ (be) to the station to see him off.

4 I will lend you the book when I _____ (do) with it.

5 _____ (you / see) my bag?

6 A: "Don't forget to pay the gas bill."

   B: "I _____ (already / do) it."

7 Jerry gave me his address, but I _____ (lose) it.

8 Where is the newspaper? What _____ (you / do) with it?

Listen to a Conversation

Try to complete the conversation with expressions from the chart below. Then listen and check your answers.

Travel Consultant : Good morning. **1**_____

Rod : We're having a great time!

Travel Consultant : Tell me about it! **2**_____

Rod : Well, we went to the top of the Empire State Building. That was the first thing we did. It's right in the center of New York!

You can see the whole city from there.

Travel Consultant : **3**_____

Rod : Yeah, we have already. We took a boat there.

It was wonderful. Crowded, but fantastic. That was yesterday. This morning we're going to take a walk around Central Park, then this afternoon we're going shopping on Fifth Avenue.

Tomorrow we're going to visit Greenwich Village and Chinatown.

Travel Consultant : Wow! You're busy!

And what about Rockefeller Center like I suggested?

4_____

Rod : No, not yet. It's on Fifth Avenue.

We're going to go there tomorrow afternoon and go ice-skating.

Travel Consultant : Tomorrow's your last night.

5_____

Rod : Well, we're going to see a Broadway show, but we haven't decided what to see yet.

Travel Consultant : You're so lucky!

Rod : Thank you for your suggestions. See you soon!

Have you been there yet?

Have you had a pleasant trip?

Have you seen the Statue of Liberty yet?

What are you going to do on your last night?

What have you done so far?

Listening Tips

The underlined syllable(s) in the words below all have vowels with a schwa sound. Can all vowels be pronounced with the schwa sound?

(* The schwa is an unstressed vowel sound. It is the most common vowel sound in English.)

int<u>ro</u>duce	*ex.* Please introduce us.
f<u>a</u>mili<u>ar</u>	*ex.* You look familiar.
t<u>o</u>geth<u>er</u>	*ex.* Let's get together soon.
prom<u>i</u>se	*ex.* I promise I'll be there.
s<u>u</u>ccess	*ex.* The business was a success.

Listen and underline the schwa sound in these words.

1 pleasant   2 wonderful

3 crowded   4 fantastic

5 yesterday   6 afternoon

7 tomorrow   8 suggest

9 avenue   10 decide

Listen the following each conversation and choose the answer.

1 Why will the couple go early to the event?

    (a) To meet some friends   (b) To get a parking place

    (c) To take some photographs   (d) To choose the best place to sit

2 What is the man looking for?

    (a) A mall   (b) A hotel

    (c) A restaurant   (d) A movie theater

3–5 What does the man want to do?

    (a) Cash a traveler's check   (b) Withdraw some money

    (c) Pay a bill   (d) Make a deposit

What does the woman need to see?

    (a) The man's bank book   (b) A proof of purchase

    (c) A guarantee   (d) Some form of identification

What does the man show her?

    (a) His passport   (b) His driver's license

    (c) His student ID card   (d) His credit card

Speaking Spot   Role-play

*** Thank A(a person) for B(reason: noun or -ing)

Thank you for your suggestions.

Thank you for kind cooperation.

Thank you for helping me with this.

Thanks for your advice.

○────

Thank you for your help.

Thank you for your assistance.

Thank you for your time.

Thank you all for your excellent work.

Thank you once again for your generosity.

Thank you once again for your continued patronage.

○────

Thank you for calling.

Thank you for ordering our products.

Thank you for choosing Starlight Internet Service.

Thank you for reminding me of today's meeting.

Thank you for doing business with our company.

Thanks for letting me know.

Conversation Tips

Look at the examples. There are two suffixes used to make a verb into a noun.

suggest － suggestion

excite － excitement

ex. What about Rockefeller Center I've suggested?

ex. Thank for your <u>suggestions</u>.

ex. The two groups agreed to cooperate with each other.

ex. Thank for your kind <u>cooperation</u>.

Write the noun forms of these verbs in the correct category.

(1) −ment	(2) −tion

1 achieve   2 celebrate   3 educate   4 explore   5 excite

6 imagine   7 govern   8 manage   9 cooperate   10 translate

Writing Tips

Present Perfect Simple + yet, still / already

(1) "Yet / still" are used when something is expected to happen but (probably) has not happened.

　① "Yet" is usually used in negative sentences and questions.

　　"Yet" always goes at the end of the sentences.

　　ex. She hasn't done a lot of editing <u>yet</u>.

　　ex. Have you done any editing <u>yet</u>?

　② "Still" is used in negative sentences with the present perfect simple. It can also be used in affirmative sentences and questions with other tenses. "Still" goes between the auxiliary and the main verb.

　　ex. He <u>still</u> hasn't quit his day job.

　　ex. He's <u>still</u> working.

　　ex. Are they <u>still</u> here?

(2) "Already" is used when something has happened sooner than expected. "Already" can go between the auxiliary and the main verb or at the end of the sentences.

　　ex. I've <u>already</u> written and directed one movie.

ex. I've written and directed one movie <u>already</u>.

Put the adverb in the correct place in each sentence.

1 Have you watched the program? (yet)

2 It's 3:00 p.m. and Jane hasn't finished the editing work. (still)

3 Katie's been in three movies. (already)

4 I'm hungry. It's 10:30 a.m. and I haven't had breakfast. (still)

5 Let's go to the movie. I haven't seen the new one at the Central Theater. (yet)

Do It Yourself

Complete the conversation using the present perfect simple.

A : Tim, **1**_____ (you / call / David / yet)

B : No, I **2**_____ (not / call / him / yet), but I

3_____ (already / talk) to Jack and Jill.

A : Good. I **4**_____ (still / not / hear from) Katie about that

new project.

B : I **5**_____ (already / talk / to / her) about it. There's a note

on your desk.

On tour:

Shopping

Building Vocabulary

Match the words with the same meaning.

1. **look for** •

   • ⓐ not mixed with anything else; with nothing added

2. **shirt** •

   • ⓑ to hope for something; to expect something

3. **go with** •

   • ⓒ a piece of clothing (usually for men), worn on the upper part of the body, made of light cloth, with sleeves and usually with a collar and buttons down the front

4. **suit** •

   • ⓓ a room or cubicle in a shop[store] where you can put on clothes to see how they look

5. **pure** •

   • ⓔ a small plastic card that you can use to buy goods and services and pay for them later

6. **cotton** •

   • ⓕ one of a number of standard measurements in which clothes, shoes and other goods are made and sold

7. **try on** •

   • ⓖ a plant grown in warm countries for the soft white hairs around its seeds that are used to make cloth and thread

8. **fitting room** •

   • ⓗ match

9. **size** •

   • ⓘ to put on a piece of clothing to see if it fits and how it looks

10. **credit card** •

   • ⓙ a set of clothes made of the same cloth, including a jacket and trousers[pants] or a skirt

Reading an Article

Read the article and answer the following questions.

Trentwood Casino Grand Opening

The Atlantic City branch of the Trentwood Casino is a superb piece of architecture of featuring twenty floors and an underground shopping mall. It is located near the center of Boardwalk Avenue, the fastest growing entertainment district in Atlantic City.

Atlantic City's Boardwalk Avenue has experienced rapid growth in the last six years, due to increased foreign investment. The Trentwood Casino is particularly proud of its luxurious setting and world-renowned hospitality. To showcase its facilities, it will be hosting a Grand Opening Fiesta on July 8, 2008.

The casino has many features, including a 5-star hotel, pampered spa, shopping mall, multi-cinema, Atlantis aquarium and children's game room. You will also find world-class restaurants like Bertoli's and Santa Antonia steak house.

- B3 Employee-Only Parking
- B2 Customer Parking
- B1 Customer Services, Lost and Found, Baby Changing Area
- 1F Snack Bars and Cafes
- 2F Shopping mall
- 3F Multi-Cinema
- 4F Aquarium (Saturday and Sunday only)
- 5F Game Room (adult supervision required for children under 10)
- 6F Casino
- 7F World Class Restaurants (open 24 hours a day)
- 8F-19F Trentwood Hotel
- 20F Pampered Spa

- Tourist information services available on the first floor.

1 What is the reason for Boardwalk Avenue's quick growth?

(a) The city has increased taxes to renovate the entire area.

(b) Local contractors have invested more money in building new hotels.

(c) Foreign businessmen have become more interested in the area.

(d) The new amusement park has attracted more tourists.

2 Where should someone go if they lose a personal item?

(a) B2   (b) B1

(c) 7F   (d) 8F

Grammar Tips

Read the following phrases and think about the meaning.

be made of	be made from	be worried about
be interested in	be excited at	be surprised at
be known for	be known as	be known to
be satisfied with	be pleased with	be covered with

ex. It's made of pure cotton.

Read and complete the sentences.

1 Tim and Lucia are both interested _____ computers. That's how they met.

2 I was surprised _____ their behavior. They usually act differently.

3 My parents are satisfied _____ the result.

4 She was pleased _____ the present.

5 We were caught _____ a shower on our way home.

6 A man is known _____ the company he keeps.

7 He is afflicted _____ a serious disease.

8 No questions were asked _____ us.

9 He is occupied _____ literary work.

10 He was absorbed _____ his studies.

Listening Spot

Listen to a Conversation

Try to complete the conversation with expressions from the chart below. Then listen and check your answers.

Salesperson : Can I help you, sir?

Barry : Yes, **1** _____

Salesperson : What color are you looking for?

Barry : I'm not sure. Blue, I think.

Salesperson : How about this one? It's made of pure cotton. Do you like it?

Barry : **2** _____

Salesperson : Well, what about this one? It's a darker blue.

Barry : Yes, I like that one much better. **3** _____

Salesperson : Yes, of course. The fitting rooms are over there. Is the size OK?

Barry : No, it's too big. **4** _____

Salesperson : I'm sorry. That's the last blue one we have.

5 _____

Barry : OK. I'll take the white. How much is it?

Salesperson : $34.99. How do you want to pay?

Barry : Can I pay by credit card?

Salesperson : Credit card's fine. Thank you very much.

But we have a smaller size in white.

Can I try it on?

Do you have a smaller size?

I'm looking for a shirt to go with my new suit.

No, it's not the right blue.

Listening Tips

Consonant sounds and vowel sounds are often linked together. There are two types of linking.

(1) **Liking between a consonant sound and a vowel sound**

    ex. We've got lots_of time.

    ex. How's_it going?

    ex. It's_an easy one.

(2) **Liking between two consonant sound**

    ex. He felt_tired all afternoon.

    ex. I have a hole in my tennis_shoe.

    ex. Let's_stay for a while.

Listen to each sentence and draw a line to connect the sounds that are linked.

1 You're just in time.

2 They are successful in business.

3 It's easier and safer.

4 I have a good deal of experience.

5 Am I in trouble?

6 Come Monday, I'll be broke.

7 If you're ready, let's go.

8 Is it time to go?

9 It's somewhere around here.

10 Does it look nice?

Further
Listening

Listen the following each conversation and choose the answer.

1 Where are the speakers?

   (a) On a bus   (b) On an airplane

   (c) In a restaurant   (d) In an automobile

2 What is the woman's problem?

   (a) Window 3 is closed.

   (b) The rate of exchange is not posted.

   (c) The bank does not accept traveler's checks

   (d) Nobody seems to know where money can be exchanged.

3 What is the man looking for?

   (a) A sales clerk   (b) The cash register

   (c) The pants department   (d) A place to try on clothes

4 What does the man want to buy?

   (a) A new car   (b) A toy for his son

   (c) A gift for his wife   (d) A jacket for himself

5 Why does the woman recommend Fifth Avenue perfume?

   (a) Price   (b) Scent

   (c) Popularity   (d) Brand name

Can I <u>try</u> it <u>on</u>?

Can I <u>try on</u> the shirt?

Can I <u>try</u> the shirt <u>on</u>?

Phrasal verbs are made up of more than one word(for example, *try on, turn on, take out* . . .). Which type of word CANNOT go after the second word in the phrasal verb?

How do you **turn on** <u>the oven</u>?

How do you **turn** <u>the oven</u> **on**?

How do you **turn** <u>it</u> **on**?

How do you turn on it? (X)

Can you **take out** <u>the sandwiches</u>?

Can you **take** <u>the sandwiches</u> **out**?

Can you **take** <u>them</u> **out**?

Can you take out them? (X)

Conversation Tips

Some phrases you can use to gently give your opinion are:

I think . . . / I guess . . . / Perhaps . . . / Maybe . . .

A : What color are you looking for?

B : I'm not sure. Blue, <u>I think</u>.

A : Is the seminar rescheduled for 6:00 this evening?

B : <u>I think</u> so.

ex. A : What is the tallest building in this town?

B : <u>I think</u> it is the Morris Hotel.

ex. A : Is that new sofa comfortable?

B : No, <u>I think</u> the old one is much better.

ex. A : Would you like to apply for that position in the marketing department?

B : <u>Maybe</u>, but when is the deadline?

ex. A : Will you be attending the dinner party?

B : <u>Probably</u>, but I may be a bit late.

Writing Tips

(1) Active : We use an active verb to say what the subject does.

ex. My grandmother <u>makes</u> her own pasta.

(2) Passive : We use a passive verb when the emphasis is on the process or action rather than the person. In other words, who or what causes the action is often unknown or unimportant.

* The passive form is ⟨be + past participle⟩

* In the passive form ⟨by + person who causes the action⟩ is often omitted.

ex. A lot of pasta <u>is made</u> in Italy.

* Simple Present VS Simple Past

ex. Tea <u>is grown</u> in India.

ex. Grapes <u>are grown</u> in France.

ex. The China <u>was taken</u> to Japan from China in 1191.

ex. Grapefruit trees <u>were taken</u> to the United States from Spain in 1840.

Do It Yourself

A. Write passive sentences.

1 A lot of rice / grow / in China

_____.

2 Potatoes / take / to Ireland from South America in 1588

_____.

3 Corn / grow / in many places in the United States today

_____.

4 The sandwich / invent / by the Earl of Sandwich in 1762

_____.

5 The first apple trees / plant / in North America in 1629

_____.

6 Today, coffee / grow / in 50 different countries

_____.

B. Rewrite the sentences in the passive.

1 They don't steam vegetables in this restaurant--they grill them.

_____.

2 In Latin America, they often make corn into flour for tortillas and other dishes.

_____.

3 In the past they grew apples and pears in Harold's area, but now they grow wheat.

_____.

4 The bakery made the cakes for the party two days ago.

_____.

Unit 1

Listening Spot

Listen to a Conversation

Travel Consultant : Hello, can I help you?

Rita : I saw your ads on the Internet and I'd like to get some information.

Travel Consultant : Where would you like to go?

Rita : I'm getting married and I'd like to go somewhere exotic.

Travel Consultant : In that case, I highly recommend Bali for you.
When do you plan to go?

Rita : I'd like to be there next month.

Travel Consultant : How long do you want to stay?

Rita : About a week. How much does it cost?

Travel Consultant : Well, it's very competitive. Would you like a brochure?

Rita : Yes, please. Thank you.

Listening Tips

1. They're from Brazil.

2. He's a teacher in Italy.

3. I'd like to play the piano.

4. He's been in Australia for three years.

5. It won't be held in Paris.

Further Listening

1. Woman : Is there a train leaving tonight for Memphis?

Man : There's one more express at, let's see . . . at nine o'clock.

Woman : Good. I'd like to a round-trip ticket, returning tomorrow evening.

2. Woman : You seem very anxious about this trip.

   Man : I am. You know, I really don't like to fly.

   Woman : Take along a good book. Try to stay calm and think about something pleasant.

3. Man : Don't you like to fly?

   Woman : Not really. I don't like to feel so closed in.

   Man : That's too bad. It sure cuts down on travel time, if you have to go very far.

4-5. Woman : You have reached international information for France. If you know the number of the area in France for which you want information, please indicate the number now. If you do not know the area, please indicate the number twelve and an operator will come on the line. If you remain on the line, this recording will play again.

Unit 2

Listening Spot

Listen to a Conversation

Travel Consultant : Good afternoon, how can I help you?

Emma : I'd like to fly to Bali with my husband on October 14th and return on October 20th.

Travel Consultant : What time do you want to leave?

Emma : Is there a flight around 7:00 o'clock in the evening?

Travel Consultant : OK, I'll check if the flight is available.
Will you be flying one-way or round trip?

Emma : Round trip, please.

Travel Consultant : (Pause) Thank you for waiting, ma'am.
There are some seats available at that time.
Economy class or first class, ma'am?

Emma	: Economy class, please.
Travel Consultant	: May I have your name and phone number, please?
Emma	: Emma Nelson, 010-3212-2588.
Travel Consultant	: All right. Do you want to pay for it now?
Emma	: Yes, thank you.

Listening Tips

1. Look at the house over there!
2. Henry, this is my mother. Mom, this is Henry.
3. This is very useful equipment.
4. Did you see Jane last week?
5. Did you get the job?

Further Listening

1. Man : If you have one available, we'd like an ocean-view room above the 10th floor.

   Woman : We have a very nice one. Of course, there's an extra charge for ocean-view rooms, sir.

   Man : That's O.K. We're on our honeymoon and we want the best.

2. Man : I'd like three seats, please, in the smoking section.

   Woman : I'm sorry. This is a domestic flight, and no smoking is permitted.

   Man : Oh, that's right. I'd like three seats together, if possible.

3-5. Man : Thank you for calling Ansett Airlines. In order to expedite your call, if you are using a touch tone phone, please press 1 now. If you have a rotary phone, please stay on the line. Please make your selection from the following menu at any time and when making your reservation, please ask about our convenient ticket delivery service. For today's flight arrival, departure, and gate information, press 1. For domestic reservations and fares in the 50 United States, press 2. For international reservations and fares, including Canada and the Caribbean, press 4. For information about Flyaway Vacations, press 5. For all other inquiries, press 6. To repeat the menu, please press 7.

Listening Spot

Listen to a Conversation

Staff : Good afternoon, ma'am. May I help you?

Alicia : Good afternoon. I'd like to check in. I'm off to New York.

Staff : May I have your ticket and passport, please?

Alicia : Here you are.

Staff : How many bags do you have?

Alicia : Two. This one to check in and a small one to carry on.

Staff : Would you mind putting your suitcases on the scale?

Alicia : No, not at all.

Staff : Thank you, ma'am. Your ticket has a further connection to San Francisco and then a return connection from there.

Alicia : Yes, I'm doing some business in New York and I'm meeting up with my husband in San Francisco for a vacation.

Staff : Which seat would you prefer, by the window or the aisle?

Alicia : Aisle side, please.

Staff : Here are your ticket, passport, boarding pass and baggage claim tags. Have a nice flight.

Alicia : Thank you very much.

Listening Tips

1. answer	2. buy	3. Christmas
4. could	5. daughter	6. eight
7. hour	8. know	9. listen
10. night	11. walk	12. write

Further Listening

1. Woman : I'd like a ticket on Flight 1-0-1 to San Diego.

   Man : What day would you like to travel?

   Woman : Thursday, the 28th.

2. Man : I'm going to need to see your passport with your airplane tickets, ma'am.

Woman : Here you are. If possible I would like a seat at the back of the plane where there are only two seats on the side.

Man : Okay. I'll check to see if there are any of those seats left.

3-5. Man : Thank you for calling Global Village Travel Hotline. For information about package tours in North America, press 1. For information about package tours in Asia, press 2. For information about package tours in West Europe, press 3. For fare and schedule information, press 4. If you would like an update on our package tours, press 5. If the line is busy, press pound and hold, your call will be answered in the order in which it was received. Thank you for using Global Village Travel.

Unit 4

Listening Spot

Listen to a Conversation

Flight Attendant : Good afternoon, ma'am. What's your seat number?

Alicia : Uh, twenty-nine K.

Flight Attendant : That's on the right side of the airplane. It's by the window. Please step this way, ma'am.

Alicia : Thank you. Where can I put my briefcase?

Flight Attendant : You may put your briefcase in this overhead compartment.

Alicia : Thank you.

Flight Attendant : We'll be taking off shortly. Would you fasten your seat belt, please?

Alicia : Sure. May I recline my seat?

Flight Attendant : I'm sorry, but not right now. You can recline it when the 'Fasten Seat Belt' sign is turned off after takeoff.

Alicia : Oh, I see. Thank you very much.

Flight Attendant : You're welcome. Enjoy your flight.

Listening Tips

1. Where will the meeting be held?

2. When can I pick up my ticket?

3. What's the deadline for sending in payment?

4. Who's responsible for the Milan project?

5. When do you plan to leave for your Asia trip?

6. Where is the Hanson file?

7. Why were you late for attending the presentation?

8. Who's the new man in the office?

Further Listening

1. Man : When will the plane land?

   Woman : The captain says we'll land as soon as we get clearance from the tower.

   Man : I hope that's soon. I have to catch a connecting flight.

2. Woman : This won't fit in the overhead compartment. What can I do?

   Man : Give it to me and I'll find a space for it at the back. You can just sit down and buckle up. We're about to pull away from the terminal.

   Woman : Thanks. Also, could you bring me a magazine?

3-5. Woman : Good evening, sir. I see you have four bags. Which would you like to take as carry on?

   Man : I'd like to check these two suitcases and carry on the two smaller bags.

   Woman : I'm afraid that due to safety regulations, we can only allow passengers one piece of carry-on baggage.

   Man : Oh, even small bags like these? Then I guess I'd better move all my valuables into just one bag.

Unit 5

Listening Spot

Listen to a Conversation

Flight Attendant : Excuse me, ma'am. We're going to serve your dinner now. Would you please lower your tray table?

Cecilia : Sure. What kinds of meals do you have today?

Flight Attendant : We have beef, fish and chicken.

Cecilia : What's the fish?

Flight Attendant : It's tuna.

Cecilia : Chicken, please.

Flight Attendant : Anything to drink?

Cecilia : Yes. Water, please.

Flight Attendant : What kind of water would you like, still or sparkling?

Cecilia : Evian, please.

Flight Attendant : I'm sorry, but we don't have any Evian.
Any other water besides Evian?

Cecilia : Well, I want to have some mineral water.

Flight Attendant : Here you are. If you need some more water, please let me know
right away.

Cecilia : Thank you. I'll do that.

Listening Tips

1. There aren't any sandwiches.

2. Do you have a good dictionary?

3. I have some photos of my dog.

4. I have a lot of books.

5. How many students are there in this class?

6. Next to my house there's a park.

Further Listening

1. Man : Could I get another cup of coffee?

   Woman : Sorry, sir, we're on our final approach now.

   Man : Oh, in that case I'd better fasten my seat belt.

2. Woman : How would you like your coffee, sir?

   Man : With cream, please. No sugar.

   Woman : I'll be right back.

3. Man : Ma'am, what kind of soft drinks do you have?

   Woman : We have cola, lemonade, and milk shakes and, of course, coffee and tea.

   Man : I'll have some lemonade, please.

4-5. Man : This is your captain speaking. Welcome aboard Thai Airlines Flight 302 to Tokyo. We have reached our cruising altitude of thirty-five thousand feet. Our flying time will be fourteen hours. We're estimating our time of arrival at Tokyo International Airport at around 10 p.m. In a few minutes, our flight attendants will serve food and beverages. And I'd like you to sit back, relax and enjoy your trip, thank you.

Unit 6

Listening Spot

Listen to a Conversation

Immigration Officer : Could I see your passport, please?

Jakob : Yes, there you go.

Immigration Officer : From Taiwan? What's the purpose of your trip?

Jakob : On business

Immigration Officer : Excuse me, but what kind of business?

Jakob : I'm doing import and export business. We do some business with U.S. companies.

Immigration Officer : How long are you staying in the United States?

Jakob : About two weeks.

Immigration Officer : Do you have any prohibited items?

Jakob : No, I don't.

Immigration Officer : Okay. That's all. Welcome to the United States, and enjoy your stay.

Jakob : Thank you.

Listening Tips

1. I worked all day, from morning until night.

2. Twelve hours in the cotton fields, and I only earned $4 a day.

3. At the time, I hated that job.

4. But I loved the poems in my head.

5. I really wanted to learn to read and write.

6. When I was twenty, I <u>married</u> Harriert.

7. So I <u>looked</u> after my family alone.

Further Listening

1-3. Man : Excuse me. Could I have another glass of water? I'm so thirsty.

Woman : Sorry, sir, but we're on our final approach now. We just latched all the beverage carts and we are getting ready for descending now.

Man : Oh, I'd better buckle my seat belt and sit still. You just go ahead with what you're doing. Sorry.

Woman : Thank you for your cooperation. I'll try to give you some drink in twenty minutes.

4-6. Woman : Welcome to Vancouver. May I see your passport please?

Man : Yes, here it is.

Woman : Are you visiting our country on business or for pleasure?

Man : I'll be doing business for three days, then I'll be sightseeing for another three.

Unit 7

Listening Spot

Listen to a Conversation

George : I've just arrived from Air Canada, but my luggage doesn't seem to be here.

Officer : What flight were you on?

George : Air Canada flight 705.

Officer : Right, that's Carousel 3, isn't it?

George : Yes, I waited there for about an hour. All the other passengers picked up their bags, but mine wasn't there.

Officer : One lost bag. Is it a suitcase?

George : Yes, a brown one.

Officer : Can you describe it, please?

George : It's a brown leather bag with a shoulder strap.

Officer : Could you fill out this form? We'll do our best to get it back, sir.

George : Thank you very much.

Officer : Tell me which hotel you're staying at. Then we'll call you there as soon as we have some information.

George : Okay. I hope to hear from you soon.

Listening Tips

1. I can speak French, but I can't speak Korean.

2. He can't dance, but he can sing.

3. They can ski, but they can't swim.

4. We can dance and we can sing.

5. I can't use a computer.

6. Were they at the party?

7. I'm sorry. I can't go to the party.

8. She wasn't at home.

9. He could play chess when he was five.

10. I can speak English very well.

Further Listening

1. Woman : Excuse me. Can you direct us to the Baggage Claim Section?

   Man : It's at that corner of the hallway. Go down straight and turn right at the second store.

   Woman : Thank you. I'm sure we'll find it.

2-4. Woman : I'm sorry, sir, but the flight to Boston has been delayed indefinitely due to weather conditions there.

   Man : Oh no. I suppose you're talking about the blizzard? What am I going to do? I have to be there by tomorrow afternoon for my workshop. I'm the one to give the presentation Woman : It's possible that the snow could stop falling a little later and you'll be able to catch the flight out. If you wait at the lounge over there, we'll let you know updated weather forecast.

   Man : Okay, I just hope things will work out for me.

Listening Spot

Listen to a Conversation

Customs officer : Do you have anything to declare?

Rick : No, I have nothing to declare.

Customs officer : Would you please open your suitcase?

Rick : Sure, why not?

Customs officer : Do you have any cigarettes, liquor or gifts?

Rick : Yes, I've one pack of ginseng tea and two bottles of honey.
They're all for my parents living in Denver.

Customs officer : How much did it cost?

Rick : 120 dollars.

Customs officer : Do you have a receipt for it?

Rick : Yes, of course. Here it is.

Customs officer : Okay. You may close your suitcase now.
Have a pleasant trip.

Rick : Thank you. Bye.

Listening Tips

1. That's five dollars and fifty cents, please.
2. You can get it for only ten dollars.
3. Here's seventy-five cents.
4. A grilled beef sandwich is only three-ninety.
5. A hundred dollars for that is very expensive!
6. That's seven-fifty, not seven-fifteen.

Further Listening

1. Man : I don't have a reservation, but I need to get to Boston as soon as possible.
When is your next departure?

   Woman : Today might be your lucky day. There's a flight in 45 minutes that isn't full.

Man : Great. Here's my credit card. Get me a seat.

2. Man : You need a boarding pass to go beyond this point.

Woman : I realize that, but I want to say good-bye to my son. He's only ten.

Man : I'm sorry, Ma'am, but you'll have to say good-bye here. I can't let you past.

3. Woman : So we board the flight at 10:00, right?

Man : Yes, and the flight to London will take approximately 11 hours so you will be getting in around 9:00 local time.

Woman : The longest flight I've had before this was only 8 hours. I hope I sleep most of the way.

4-5. Woman : While you are waiting for your flight why don't you come by our duty free shopping plaza on the lower level of the airport? We have everything the world traveler could hope for including photography equipment, clothing, handbags, and so much more. Right now we are offering special discounts on local crafts produced by native villagers right here on the island of Oahu. Even if you just want to buy a special souvenir from Hawaii for a family member or friend back home, we have lots of different gift ideas to choose from.

Unit 9

Listening Spot

Listen to a Conversation

Information Officer : What can I do for you, ma'am?

Sharon : I need some directions. I'd like to do some shopping at one of the big department stores.

Information Officer : Most of the big stores are downtown.

Sharon : What's the best way to get there?

Information Officer : If you go by bus, it takes about 30 minutes.

Sharon : Is there a shuttle bus to downtown Vancouver?

Information Officer : Sure. Just go right through those doors. The shuttle bus stop is right outside.

Sharon : What about going by train?

Information Officer : The subway takes less time and the subway station isn't far from here, too.

Sharon : How do I get there?

Information Officer : You go out of the airport terminal, turn right, and it's a five-minute walk.

Sharon : OK, thanks a lot.

Information Officer : It's my pleasure, ma'am.

Listening Tips

1. We can learn how to act.

2. What do you think of the baseball club?

3. We can have a lot of fun.

4. Do you want to join the art club?

5. I'll meet you at the park.

6. Can you think of anything else?

7. Do you have to study tonight?

Further Listening

1. Man : I'm looking for the Crown Hotel.

   Woman : You need to turn right at this light. It's two blocks down, on your right.

   Man : Thanks. I've been driving around for twenty minutes trying to find it. I was about to give up.

2. Woman : What's the best way to get to the airport from here?

   Man : Our shuttle service is very convenient and leaves every 30 minutes.

   Woman : Good. That gives me some time to have lunch before I leave.

3-5. Woman : How far is it from here to the university?

   Man : About fifteen miles. By car, it takes twenty minutes.

   Woman : That's not so bad. I thought it was much further than that.

   Man : Yeah, but it takes almost an hour by bus. You have to change twice.

Listening Spot

Hotel Receptionist : Good evening, sir.

Charles : Good evening. I want to check in.

Hotel Receptionist : Do you have a reservation?

Charles : Yes, I do. My name is Charles, Santos.

Hotel Receptionist : Let me check . . . I don't have your name on the computer.

Charles : Try my company. That's LG Chemistry Company.

Hotel Receptionist : Did you say "LG Chemistry Company?" Ah, yes. I have it here.
How many nights are you staying?

Charles : For three night, October 14th to 17th.

Hotel Receptionist : Yes, a double room for three nights with an ocean view. You'll
be in Room 702--that's on the fifth floor.
How will you be paying, credit card or cash?

Charles : I'll be paying by credit card.

Hotel Receptionist : OK. I just need you to complete this registration card.

Charles : Thank you. Uh, sorry, what's the date today?

Hotel Receptionist : October 14th, 2010. You're in Room 702. Here is your key card.
The bellboy will bring up your luggage. Enjoy your stay.

Charles : Thank you very much.

1. Did you say "the soccer club"?
2. Did you say he likes video games?
3. Did you say "at the cafeteria"?
4. Did you say it's five dollars?
5. What class did he say, "literature"?
6. Did she say she wanted to see that new action movie?
7. Did you say "already have a reservation"?

Further Listening

1. Man : Good afternoon. Do you have a reservation?

   Woman : Yes, my husband and I registered under the name, Smith. We reserved a double room for three nights.

   Man : Yes, Mrs. Smith. I have it right here. Could I get you to fill out this form, please?

2. Woman : I'd like two single rooms, please.

   Man : I'm sorry. All we have left are double rooms, but I can give them to you for the same rate. Would that be O.K.?

   Woman : Of course. Thank you.

3-5. Man : Excuse me. I need to check out of my room about 30 minutes late tomorrow. I'm expecting a phone call at 10:30, and I won't be finished by 11:00. Will that be a problem?

   Woman : Not at all. Your bill has already been paid, so just leave your keys in the room.

   Man : Great. Thank you very much.

   Woman : I hope you enjoyed your stay.

Unit 11

Listening Spot

Listen to a Conversation

Waiter : Good evening. Do you have a reservation?

Steve : No, but I'm staying at this hotel. Do you have a table for two?

Waiter : Yes, here we are. Now, there's a table near the window or one out on the terrace. Which one would you prefer?

Steve : It's a bit cold today. I think I'll stay inside.

Waiter : Yes, let me show you to your table. . .

   Here is the menu. Let me tell you about our specials today.

   The fish of the day is trout and the soup is clam chowder.

Steve : What's the trout like?

Waiter : Oh, it's very nice. It's pan-fried and served with a herb sauce.

Steve : OK, I'll have the steak.

Waiter : How would you like that cooked?

Steve : Medium rare, thanks. Oh, what's that served with?

Waiter : It's served with vegetables and a mushroom sauce.

Steve : That's fine. Can I have two bottles of beer, please?

Waiter : Sure. I'll be right back with your drinks.

Listening Tips

1. Would you like a cigarette?

2. Do you like your teacher?

3. Would you like a drink?

4. Yes. I'd like a book of stamps, please.

5. Well, I like swimming very much.

6. Yes. I'd like a hamburger, please.

7. I'd like some fruit.

8. I like books by John Bunyan.

9. I'd like a new bike.

10. I like cats, but I don't like dogs.

Further Listening

1. Man : What would you like?

   Woman : I don't know. What would you recommend?

   Man : The broiled salmon is very good. It's the specialty of the house.

2. Man : May we have a table for three, please?

   Woman : Yes, but there will be a 10-minute wait.

   Man : That's fine. Can we look over a menu while we're waiting?

3-5. Woman : Good afternoon, and welcome to Frank's Fried Seafood. My name is Elizabeth, and I'll be serving you today. Here are our lunch menus and a basket of freshly baked bread. Our special today is grilled salmon with a cream sauce. If you would like to order something from our dinner menu, you certainly may, but be advised that your meal will take longer to prepare. Also, I'm afraid that our soda machine is out of order, so the only cold drinks available are water, lemonade, and iced tea. As for beer or wine, I'm sorry, but Frank's does not serve alcoholic beverages. I'll be back in a few moments to take your orders.

Unit 12

Listening Spot

Listen to a Conversation

Travel Consultant : Good morning. Have you had a pleasant trip?

Rod : We're having a great time!

Travel Consultant : Tell me about it! What have you done so far?

Rod : Well, we went to the top of the Empire State Building.
That was the first thing we did. It's right in the center of New York!
You can see the whole city from there.

Travel Consultant : Have you seen the Statue of Liberty yet?

Rod : Yeah, we have already. We took a boat there.

It was wonderful. Crowded, but fantastic. That was yesterday.
This morning we're going to take a walk around Central Park, then this afternoon we're going shopping on Fifth Avenue.
Tomorrow we're going to visit Greenwich Village and Chinatown.

Travel Consultant : Wow! You're busy!
And what about Rockefeller Center like I suggested?
Have you been there yet?

Rod : No, not yet. It's on Fifth Avenue.
We're going to go there tomorrow afternoon and go ice-skating.

Travel Consultant : Tomorrow's your last night.
What are you going to do on your last night?

Rod : Well, we're going to see a Broadway show, but we haven't decided what to see yet.

Travel Consultant : You're so lucky!

Rod : Thank you for your suggestions. See you soon!

Listening Tips

1. pleasant   2. wonderful   3. crowded

4. fantastic   5. yesterday   6. afternoon

7. tomorrow   8. suggest   9. avenue

10. decide

Further Listening

1. Woman : What time is the parade on Saturday?

   Man : At one o'clock, but we should get there early so we get seats in the shade.

   Woman : I agree, but we also want to have a good view.

2. Man : Isn't there a Greek restaurant around here somewhere?

   Woman : No, but there's one in the Village Mall. It's too far to walk. If you want to go there, you'll have to take a taxi.

   Man : Oh, I thought there was one just around the block. I'm too hungry to wait.

3-5. Man : Excuse me. Can I cash a traveler's check here?

   Woman : Yes, but I'll need to see some identification first. May I see your passport, please?

   Man : I'm afraid I don't have it on me right now. Will you accept my driver's license?

   Woman : Yes, that'll do just fine. I'll just need to make a copy of it.

Unit 13

Listening Spot

Listen to a Conversation

Salesperson : Can I help you, sir?

Barry : Yes, I'm looking for a shirt to go with my new suit.

Salesperson : What color are you looking for?

Barry : I'm not sure. Blue, I think.

Salesperson : How about this one? It's made of pure cotton. Do you like it?

Barry : No, it's not the right blue.

Salesperson : Well, what about this one? It's a darker blue.

Barry : Yes, I like that one much better. Can I try it on?

Salesperson : Yes, of course. The fitting rooms are over there. Is the size OK?

Barry : No, it's too big. Do you have a smaller size?

Salesperson : I'm sorry. That's the last blue one we have.
But we have a smaller size in white.

Barry : OK. I'll take the white. How much is it?

Salesperson : $34.99. How do you want to pay?

Barry : Can I pay by credit card?

Salesperson : Credit card's fine. Thank you very much.

Listening Tips

1. You're just in time.

2. They are successful in business.

3. It's easier and safer.

4. I have a good deal of experience.

5. Am I in trouble?

6. Come Monday, I'll be broke.

7. If you're ready, let's go.

8. Is it time to go?

9. It's somewhere around here.

10. Does it look nice?

Further Listening

1. Woman : What time will we be eating lunch?
   Man : While you were sleeping, the driver announced we'll stop at about 12:30.
   Woman : I can hardly wait. I'm starved.

2. Woman : Can I exchange traveler's checks at this window?
   Man : No, I'm sorry. You have to go to Window 3.
   Woman : Someone is confused. I went to Window 3, and the clerk there sent me here.

3. Woman : Would like to try on those pants?
   Man : Yes, where are the dressing rooms?

Woman : They're on the other side of the cash register. There, to your left.

4. Woman : Can I help you find something?

   Man   : Yes, I need a birthday present for my wife.

   Woman : Well, a bottle of a good perfume always makes a nice gift.

5. Man   : Miss, what kind of perfume do you recommend for a woman who is very, let's say, outgoing?

   Woman : Perhaps Fifth Avenue. It's one of our most popular brands.

   Man   : If other people like it, it must be good. Please give me one of those large bottles.

Unit 1

Warm-up

Building Vocabulary

1. I
2. f
3. d
4. h
5. a.
6. j
7. g
8. b
9. e
10. c.

Reading Spot

Reading an Article

1. (b) To be recognized by tour representatives
2. (d) By ship
3. (a) Copenhagen
4. (c) 3weeks

Grammar Tips

1. to go
2. to wear / wearing

3. to sit
4. living
5. to talk / to speak

Listening Spot

Listen to a Conversation

1. I'd like to get some information.
2. Where would you like to go?
3. I'd like to go somewhere exotic.
4. I'd like to be there next month.
5. Would you like a brochure?

Listening Tips

1. They're from Brazil.
2. He's a teacher in Italy.
3. I'd like to play the piano.
4. He's been in Australia for three years.
5. It won't be held in Paris.

Further Listening

1. (d) By train
2. (d) Nervous
3. (d) In airplanes
4. (d) From a country other than France
5. (a) Press a number

Writing Spot

Do It Yourself

1. I would like to buy a one-way, please.
2. I would like to stay for three days, please.
3. I would like to travel with my sister, please.
4. I would like to go to London, please.
5. I would like to make a few stops, please.
6. I would like to get some information, please.
7. I would like to leave next Friday, please.

Unit 2

Warm-up

Building Vocabulary

1. g
2. h
3. a
4. d
5. j
6. b
7. e
8. I
I. c
10. f.

Reading Spot

Reading an Article

1. (c) Vancouver
2. (a) She wants reservations made.
3. (a) Within two days

Grammar Tips

1. is
2. isn't
3. are
4. are
5. aren't

Listening Spot

Listen to a Conversation

1. Is there a flight around 7:00 o'clock in the evening?
2. Will you be flying one-way or round trip?
3. There are some seats available at that time.
4. May I have your name and phone number, please?
5. Do you want to pay for it now?

Listening Tips

1. Look at the house over there!
2. Henry, this is my mother. Mom, this is Henry.
3. This is very useful equipment.
4. Did you see Jane last week?
5. Did you get the job?

Further Listening

1. (c) He wants a room with a view.

2. (d) Smoke on board the airplane

3. (c) To speed up your call

4. (a) 1

5. (d) Ticket delivery

Writing Spot

Do It Yourself

1. There are many mistakes in the book.

2. There is fax service.

3. There is a TV and VCR in the room.

4. There is 24-hour room service.

5. There are three restaurants in the hotel.

6. There are tennis courts in yard.

7. There are people in auditorium.

Unit 3

Warm-up

Building Vocabulary

1. h

2. c

3. f

4. j

5. a.

6. I

7. b

8. d

9. g

10. e.

Reading Spot

Reading an Article

1. (a) A traveler's itinerary

2. (c) Atlanta

3. (d) 2 hours and 10 minutes

Grammar Tips

1. I'm playing

2. I'll lend

3. I'm throwing

4. Are you doing

5. I'll take

Listening Spot

Listen to a Conversation

1. I'd like to check in.

2. How many bags do you have?

3. Would you mind putting your suitcases on the scale?

4. No, not at all.

5. Which seat would you prefer, by the window or the aisle?

Listening Tips

1. answer → w

2. buy → u

3. Christmas → t

4. could → l

5. daughter → gh

6. eight → gh

7. hour → h

8. know → k

9. listen → t

10. night → gh

11. walk → l

12. write → w

Further Listening

1. (b) Go to San Diego

2. (d) Assign a seat

3. (b) Press 2

4. (d) 4

5. (d) Press # and hold

Writing Spot

Do It Yourself

1. She gave up trying to find her cell phone.

2. Although Dave is 65 years old, he wants to go on working.

3. He tried to avoid answering the phone.

4. She gave up applying for the job yesterday.

5. Have you finished your project?

6. He is considering quitting smoking now.

7. The boy denied stealing a toy in the department store.

Unit 4

Warm-up

Building Vocabulary

1. d

2. h

3. I

4. a

5. f

6. j

7. c

8. g

9. b

10. e

Reading Spot

Reading an Article

1. (b) Passengers must fly once a month for 12 months.

2. (d) It doesn't matter how far you fly.

3. (c) A maximum of 4

4. (b) By calling a special phone line or downloading the form

Grammar Tips

1. will be staying

2. will be playing

3. will have finished

4. will have traveled

5. will be working

Listening Spot

Listen to a Conversation

1. What's your seat number?

2. Where can I put my briefcase?

3. We'll be taking off shortly.

4. May I recline my seat?

5. Enjoy your flight.

Listening Tips

1. Where

2. When

3. What

4. Who

5. When

6. Where

7. Why

8. Who

Further Listening

1. (d) He has another plane to catch.

2. (b) On an airplane

3. (c) Airport check-in desk clerk

4. (d) Half of them

5. (d) Put all his important items together

Speaking Spot

Conversation Tips

1. Can you[Could you]

2. Can you[Could you]

3. Can I[Could I]

4. Can you[Could you]

5. Can you[Could you]

6. Can I[Could I]

Writing Spot

Do It Yourself

1. I'll be paying for the bill with Visa card.

2. She'll be staying for two nights.

3. I'll be using my cell phone daily.

4. I'll be meeting some co-workers for

dinner.

5. He'll be needing his briefcase right now.

6. I'll be paying with cash.

7. We'll be needing day care tomorrow afternoon.

Unit 5

Warm-up

Building Vocabulary

1. h

2. g

3. a

4. I

5. c

6. j

7. f

8. b

9. d

10. e.

Reading Spot

Reading an Article

1. (d) "Loose Change Found on Planes"

2. (c) Information provided by one airline

3. (a) International passengers discard unwanted coins.

Grammar Tips

1. any, some

2. some

3. some

4. any

5. any

6. any

7. some

8. any

Listening Spot

Listen to a Conversation

1. Would you please lower your tray table?

2. What kinds of meals do you have today?

3. What's the fish?

4. What kind of water would you like, still ar sparking?

5. Any other water besides Evian?

Listening Tips

1. There aren't any sandwiches.

2. Do you have a good dictionary?

3. I have some photos of my dog.

4. I have a lot of books.

5. How many students are there in this class?

6. Next to my house there's a park.

Further Listening

1. (b) On an airplane

2. (c) Ordering coffee

3. (c) Something to drink

4. (b) A pilot

5. (c) In fourteen hours

Writing Spot

Do It Yourself

2. I'm sorry, we don't have any cheese, but we do have some nuts.

3. I'm sorry, we don't have any tables on the terrace, but we do have some tables inside the restaurant.

4. I'm sorry, we don't have any decaffeinated coffee, but we do have some regular coffee.

5. I'm sorry, we don't have any roast chicken, but we do have some roast beef.

6. I'm sorry, we don't have any white wine, but we do have some red wine.

7. I'm sorry, we don't have any ice cream, but we do have some whipping cream.

Unit 6

Warm-up

Building Vocabulary

1. g

2. h

3. j

4. a

5. c

6. e

7. I

8. f

9. b

10. d.

Reading Spot

Reading an Article

1. (d) Foreign investors
2. (a) The demolition of the existing terminal

Grammar Tips

1. exhausted
2. waiting
3. taken
4. burning
5. singing
6. lighted
7. made
8. writing
9. fallen
10. developed, printed

Listening Spot

Listen to a Conversation

1. there you go.
2. On business
3. I'm doing import and export business.
4. How long are you staying in the United States?
5. Do you have any prohibited items?

Listening Tips

1. /t/
2. /d/
3. /id/
4. /d/
5. /id/
6. /d/
7. /t/

Further Listening

1. (b) In a plane
2. (c) She can't serve water now.
3. (a) Twenty minutes later
4. (b) At the airport
5. (d) For business and pleasure
6. (c) Six days

Writing Spot

Do It Yourself

1. Could I have your room key, please?
2. Could you write your address, please?
3. Could you fill out this form, please?
4. Could you wait here, please?
5. Could you sign on the bottom line, please?
6. Could you wait over there, please?

Unit 7

Warm-up

Building Vocabulary

1. d
2. b
3. g

4. I

5. f

6. e

7. j

8. h

9. a

10. c.

Reading Spot

Reading an Article

1. (d) Fill out an application for compensation at the ticket counter

2. (a) The insurance airlines provide is often not enough.

3. (d) By paying a service fee at the ticket counter

Grammar Tips

1. How long ago did you move to the United States

2. I've been here for 15 years

3. Did you go to Venezuela last year

4. I haven't gone to Venezuela since 1997

Listening Spot

Listen to a Conversation

1. What flight were you on?

2. that's Carousel 3, isn't it?

3. Is it a suitcase?

4. It's a brown leather bag with a shoulder strap.

5. Tell me which hotel you're staying at.

Listening Tips

1. can / can't

2. can't / can

3. can / can't

4. can / can

5. I can't use a computer.

6. Were they at the party?

7. I'm sorry. I can't go to the party.

8. She wasn't at home.

9. He could play chess when he was five.

10. I can speak English very well.

Further Listening

1. (b) Where to find their bags

2. (b) Change in flight schedule

3. (b) He can't leave on schedule.

4. (c) An airline receptionist

Writing Spot

Writing Tips

1. g

2. c

3. d

4. f

5. h

6. a

7. b

8. e

Do It Yourself

1. aren't you

2. I am

3. isn't he

4. he is

5. did you

6. I didn't

7. did we

Unit 8

Warm-up

Building Vocabulary

1. j
2. h
3. a
4. c
5. g
6. I
7. d
8. e
9. b
10. f.

Reading Spot

Reading an Article

1. (c) There will be one more daily flight to Buffalo from County Airport.
2. (b) Two
3. (a) He works for the Metro Airport Authority.
4. (c) It was desired by local business travelers.

Grammar Tips

1. piece
2. glass
3. pair
4. suit
5. spoonfuls
6. bottles

Listening Spot

Listen to a Conversation

1. Do you have anything to declare?
2. Sure, why not?
3. Do you have any cigarettes, liquor or gifts?
4. How much did it cost?
5. Do you have a receipt for it?

Listening Tips

1. $5.50
2. $10
3. $0.75
4. $3.90
5. $100
6. $7.50

Further Listening

1. (c) At an airline desk
2. (c) She did not have a boarding pass.
3. (d) Eleven hours
4. (a) In an airport
5. (b) Duty Free Alcohol

Writing Spot

1. Look at the boy and his dog running over there.

2. I was awakened by a bell ringing.

3. Do you know the woman talking to Tom?

4. I have a large bedroom overlooking the garden.

5. Some of the people invited to the party can't come.

6. A receptionist working at night won a lotto.

7. A waiter serving in the restaurant passed entrance exams for college.

Unit 9

Warm-up

Building Vocabulary

1. b
2. e
3. g
4. a
5. h
6. j
7. I
8. c
9. f
10. d.

Reading Spot

Reading an Article

1. (b) The new meal policy of Kingfisher Airlines

2. (c) It has joined other airlines in attempting to cut losses.

3. (a) Coffee

Grammar Tips

1. bigger
2. less expensive
3. Electra / heavier
4. Electra / newer
5. Sonic / smaller

Listening Spot

Listen to a Conversation

1. I need some directions.
2. What's the best way to get there?
3. Is there a shuttle bus to downtown Vancouver?
4. What about going by train?
5. How do I get there?

Listening Tips

1. to
2. of
3. of
4. to
5. at
6. of
7. to

Further Listening

1. (d) Directions

2. (a) Every half hour

3. (c) Twenty minutes

4. (b) She thought the university was farther.

5. (b) The bus route is not direct.

Writing Spot

Do It Yourself

1. The taxi to the airport takes fifteen minutes.

2. The trip to the National Museum / takes half an hour.

3. It takes less time by bicycle.

4. A bus takes three hours because of the traffic.

5. How long does it take to get there?

6. The trip to the zoo takes one and half an hour.

7. The walk to the subway station takes ten minutes.

Unit 10

Warm-up

Building Vocabulary

1. g
2. I
3. h
4. a
5. j
6. e

7. c

8. d

9. b

10. f

Reading Spot

Reading an Article

1. (c) Its luxury

2. (b) The hotel is very comfortable.

Grammar Tips

A

1. first
2. second
3. third
4. fourth
5. fifth
6. sixth
7. tenth
8. twelfth
9. thirteenth
10. sixteenth
11. seventeenth
12. twentieth
13. twenty-first
14. thirtieth
15. thirty-first

B

1. April first
2. March second
3. September seventeenth
4. November nineteenth

5. June twenty-third

6. February twenty-ninth, nineteen seventy-six

7. December nineteenth, nineteen eight-three

8. October third, nineteen ninety-nine

9. May thirty-first, two thousand

10. July fifteenth, two thousand four

Listening Spot

Listen to a Conversation

1. Do you have a reservation?

2. Try my company.

3. How many nights are you staying?

4. How will you be paying, credit card or cash?

5. what's the date today?

Listening Tips

1. checking

2. surprised

3. checking

4. surprised

5. checking

6. surprised

7. checking

Further Listening

1. (b) A front desk clerk

2. (b) Two double rooms

3. (b) At a hotel

4. (b) He is expecting a phone call.

5. (a) 11:30

Writing Spot

Writing Tips

1. many

2. many

3. much

4. many

5. much

6. many

7. much

Do It Yourself

1. How many books do you want?

2. I don't like ice cream.

3. Can I have some bread, please?

4. I'd like a sandwich.

5. I don't have much milk left.

6. I'd like some fruit, please.

7. How much money do you have?

8. We have much homework today.

Unit 11

Warm-up

Building Vocabulary

1. j

2. a

3. f

4. g

5. b

6. h

7. I

8. c

9. e

10. d.

Reading Spot

Reading an Article

1. (c) Soft drinks

2. (c) Fruit

3. (d) Salad and vegetable

Grammar Tips

A

well-known / absent-minded / To Do /
full-time / brand-new / well-dressed /
left-handed / right-handed

B

1. short-sleeved

2. good-looking

3. right-handed

4. full-time

5. First-class

6. brand-new

Listening Spot

Listen to a Conversation

1. Do you have a table for two?

2. Which one would you prefer?

3. Let me tell you about our specials today.

4. What's the trout like?

5. what's that served with?

Listening Tips

1. Would you like a cigarette?

2. Do you like your teacher?

3. Would you like a drink?

4. Yes. I'd like a book of stamps, please.

5. Well, I like swimming very much.

6. Yes. I'd like a hamburger, please.

7. I'd like some fruit.

8. I like books by John Bunyan.

9. I'd like a new bike.

10. I like cats, but I don't like dogs.

Further Listening

1. (c) In a restaurant

2. (d) See what the restaurant serves

3. (d) Soda

4. (d) The food will take longer.

5. (d) None

Speaking Spot

Conversation Tips

1. What's the soup like?

2. What's the weather like?

3. What's the restaurant like?

4. What's the local beer like?

5. What are the beaches like?

6. What's the music like?

7. What are the facilities like?

Writing Spot

1. Let me show you the menu.

2. Let me give you the table near the window.

3. Let me show you how to use the fax machine.

4. Let me take you to the shopping mall.

5. Let me take your bags to your room.

6. Let me check the air conditioning.

7. Let me read the TV program guide to you.

Unit 12

Warm-up

Building Vocabulary

1. e
2. I
3. j
4. a
5. c
6. h
7. g
8. b
9. f
10. d

Reading Spot

Reading an Article

1. (c) On March 10

2. (a) Free tickets to a play

Grammar Tips

1. have just finished
2. has been
3. have been
4. have done
5. Have you seen
6. have already done
7. have lost
8. have you done

Listening Spot

Listen to a Conversation

1. Have you had a pleasant trip?

2. What have you done so far?

3. Have you seen the Statue of Liberty yet?

4. Have you been there yet?

5. What are you going to do on your last night?

Listening Tips

1. pleasant
2. wonderful
3. crowded
4. fantastic
5. yesterday
6. afternoon
7. tomorrow
8. suggest
9. avenue
10. decide

Further Listening

1. (d) To choose the best place to sit

2. (c) A restaurant

3. (a) Cash a traveler's check

4. (d) Some form of identification

5. (b) His driver's license

Speaking Spot

Conversation Tips

(1) -ment : achievement / excitement / government / management

(2) -tion : celebration / education / exploration / imagination / cooperation / translation

Writing Spot

Writing Tips

1. Have you watched the program▼? (yet)

2. It's 3:00 p.m. and Jane ▼ hasn't finished the editing work. (still)

3. Katie's ▼ been in three movies▼. (already)

4. I'm hungry. It's 10:30 a.m. and I ▼ haven't had breakfast. (still)

5. Let's go to the movie. I haven't seen the new one at the Central Theater▼. (yet)

Do It Yourself

1. Have you called David yet?

2. have not called him yet

3. have already talked

4. still have not heard from

5. have already talked to her

Unit 13

Warm-up

Building Vocabulary

1. b

2. c

3. h

4. j

5. a

6. g

7. I

8. d

9. f

10. e

Reading Spot

Reading an Article

1. (c) Foreign businessmen have become more interested in the area.

2. (b) B1

Grammar Tips

1. in

2. at

3. with

4. with

5. in

6. for

7. with

8. of

9. with

10. in

Listen to a Conversation

1. I'm looking for a shirt to go with my new suit.

2. No, it's not the right blue.

3. Can I try it on?

4. Do you have a smaller size?

5. But we have a smaller size in white.

Listening Tips

1. You're just in time.

2. They are successful in business.

3. It's easier and safer.

4. I have a good deal of experience.

5. Am I in trouble?

6. Come Monday, I'll be broke.

7. If you're ready, let's go.

8. Is it time to go?

9. It's somewhere around here.

10. Does it look nice?

Further Listening

1. (a) On a bus

2. (d) Nobody seems to know where money can be exchanged.

3. (d) A place to try on clothes

4. (c) A gift for his wife

5. (c) Popularity

Writing Spot

Do It Yourself

A

1. A lot of rice is grown in China.

2. Potatoes were taken to Ireland from South America in 1588.

3. Corn is grown in many places in the United States today.

4. The sandwich was invented by the Earl of Sandwich in 1762.

5. The first apple trees were planted in North America in 1629.

6. Today, coffee is grown in 50 different countries.

B

1. Vegetables aren't steamed in this restaurant— they are grilled.

2. In Latin America, corn is often made into flour for tortillas and other dishes.

3. In the past apples and pears were grown in Harold's area, but now wheat is grown.

4. The cake were made (by the bakery) for the party two days ago.
OR The cakes for the party were made by the bakery) two days ago.

저자약력

신동선

· 한양대학교 영어영문학과 문학박사(르네상스 영문학)
· 한양대학교 영어영문학과 문학석사
· 한양대학교 영어영문학과 학사
· 현) 숭의여자대학교 관광과 겸임교수
　　한양대학교, 경기대학교, 충북대학교, 세종사이버대학교 강사

주요논문
· 초기 도시희극으로서의 『구두장이의 휴일』과 『윈저의 즐거운 아내들』 연구 –
　한량을 중심으로(박사학위논문, 2007년 2월)
· *Antony and Cleoparta* : 비극내의 희비극적 양상 연구(석사학위논문, 1998년 2월)

박상현

· 한양대학교 대학원 관광학과 박사
· 한양대학교 대학원 관광학과 석사
· 국제영어대학원 대학교 영어지도학과 석사
· 한양사이버대학교 호텔관광경영학과 교수
· 관광종사원 국가자격시험 심사위원
· 한국호텔관광학회 이사

저서
· Applying Importance-Satisfaction Analysis to Tourism English Course at College
　외 논문 및 교재 다수

자격증 및 수료증
· 관광통역안내사(영어) 자격 취득
· Hanyang-Oregon TESOL 과정 수료

저자와의
합의하에
인지첩부
생략

Tourism English A to Z

2010년 11월 30일 초 판 1쇄 발행
2020년 3월 10일 제2판 1쇄 발행

지은이 신동선 · 박상현
펴낸이 진욱상
펴낸곳 백산출판사
교　정 편집부
본문디자인 오행복
표지디자인 오정은

등　록 1974년 1월 9일 제406-1974-000001호
주　소 경기도 파주시 회동길 370(백산빌딩 3층)
전　화 02-914-1621(代)
팩　스 031-955-9911
이메일 edit@ibaeksan.kr
홈페이지 www.ibaeksan.kr

ISBN 979-11-5763-225-1 93740
값 17,000원